Amish Easter
Coloring Book & Writing Prompts
for kids and adults

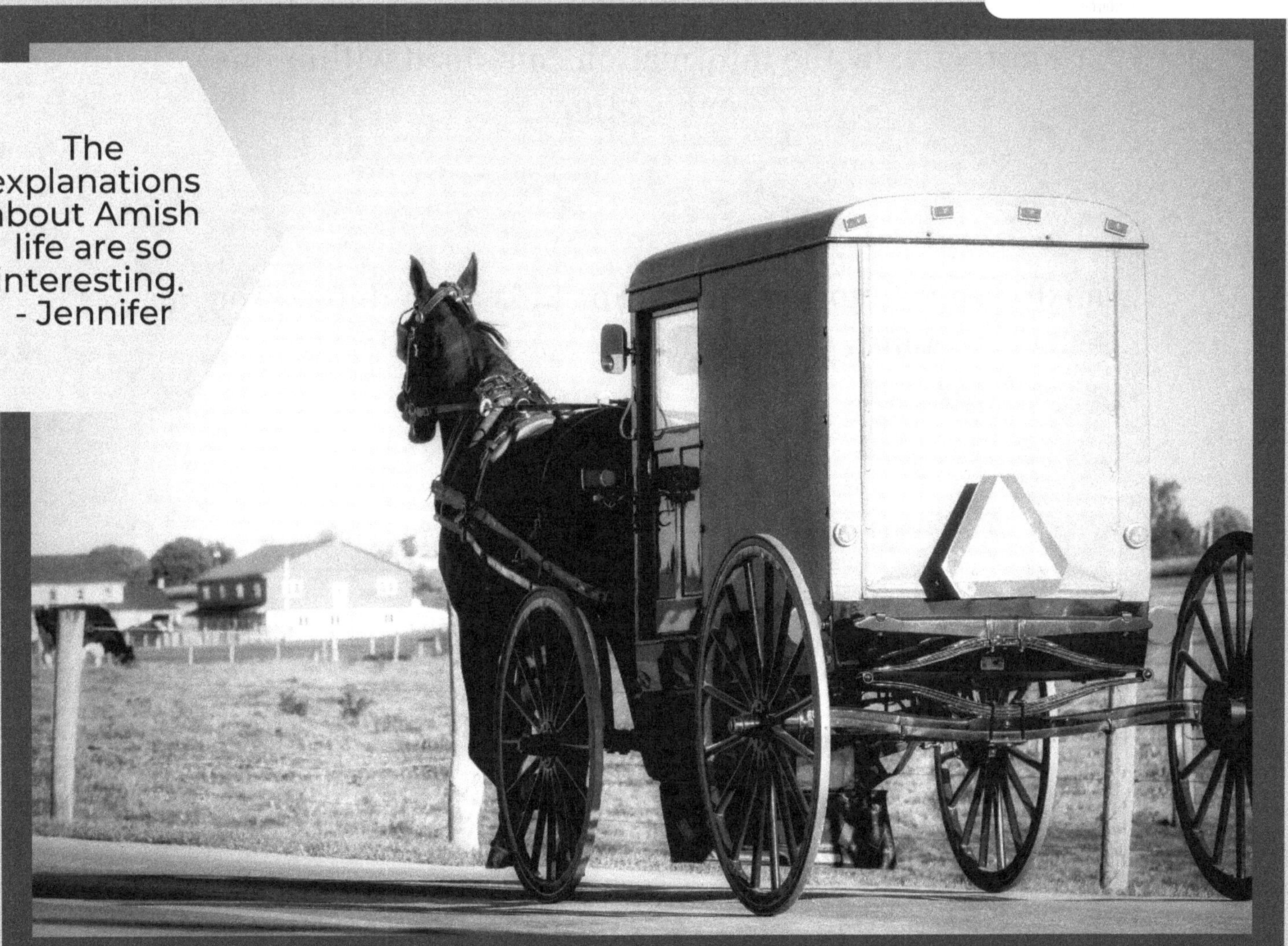

> The explanations about Amish life are so interesting.
> - Jennifer

MARY K. MILLER

Copyright © 2020 Mary K. Miller. All rights reserved.

No part of this publication may be reproduced, stored or transmitted in whole or in part in any form or by any means, including electronic, mechanical, photographic, photocopying or recording or by any information storage or retrieval system, without prior written permission of the publisher or copyright owner. The author(s) and publisher assume neither responsibility nor liability to any person or entity for any loss or damage caused, or alleged to have been caused, directly or indirectly, by the information contained within this publication.

Amish Easter Coloring Book - For Kids and Adults: From an Amish Grandmother / Mary K. Miller.

ISBN: 9798581028124

Printed in the United States of America

For more from Mary, visit her author page: www.amzn.to/2JUGdTR

He is not here; he has risen! Remember how he told you, while he was still with you in Galilee: "The Son of Man must be delivered over to the hands of sinners, be crucified and on the third day be raised again."

- Luke 24:6-7

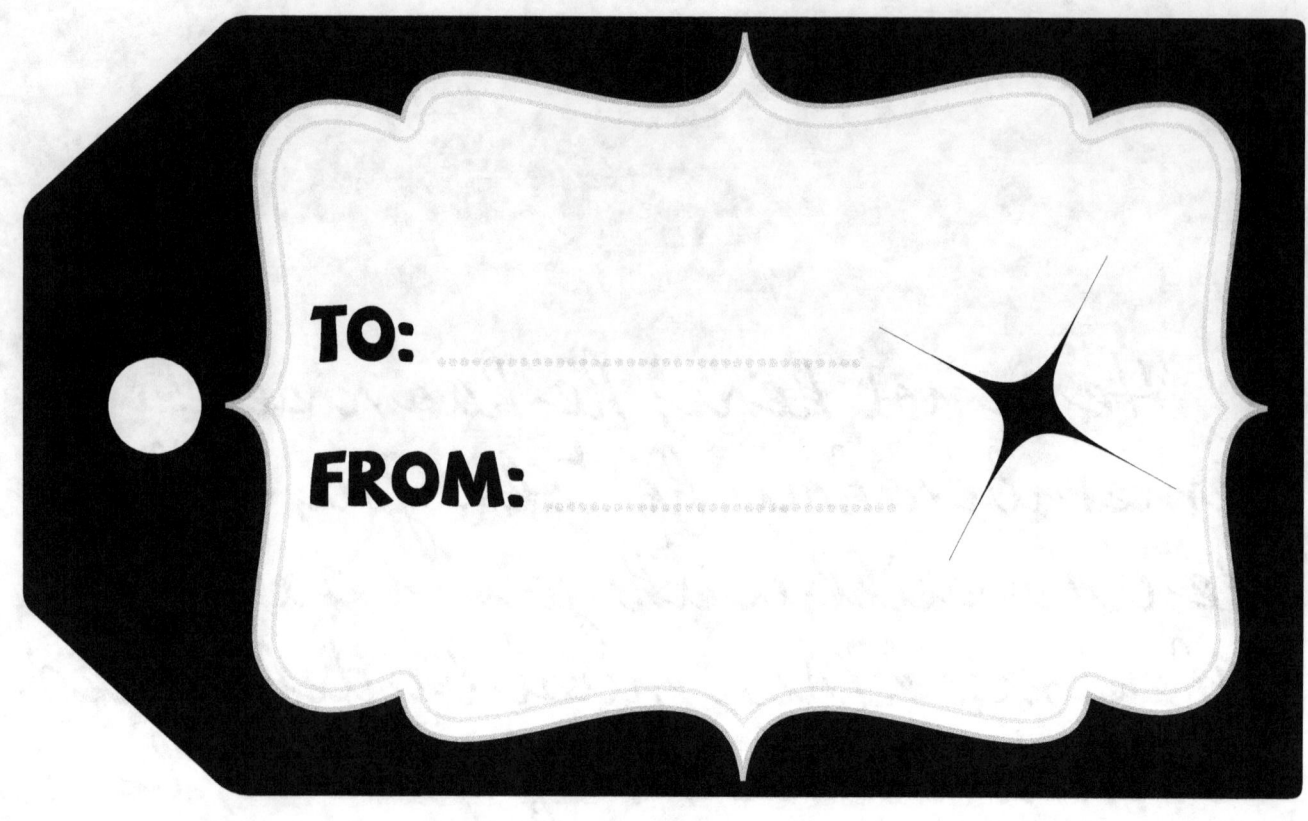

WELCOME

Thank you for your purchase. I hope you find this coloring book enjoyable.

I am a traditional Amish wife, mother of 9 children, and grandmother of 4 children. Now that all of my children are grown, I'm sharing my faith and traditions with others through useful items like this book.

As you go through each section, you will learn about how the Amish celebrate Easter.

Each popular holiday image series is prefaced with a paragraph about the role it plays in my home.

Happy Easter and may God bless you!

Mary K. Miller

For more items, visit www.amzn.to/2JUGdTR

EGG

EGG

Some Amish allow their children to dye Easter eggs and have Easter egg hunts at home and at school. Some communities also allow school children to color pictures of secular Easter images and hang them up in the Amish schoolhouse for decoration.

But other Amish communities forbid all non-religious pictures and activities.

Dying eggs and taking turns to hide and hunt for them in the yard was one of my children's, and now grandchildren's, favorite activities of the year.

WRITING PROMPT: What does an egg mean to you?

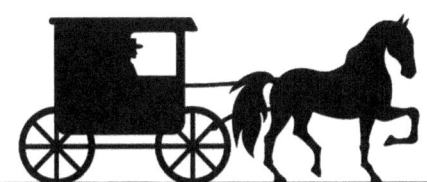

WRITING PROMPT

continued

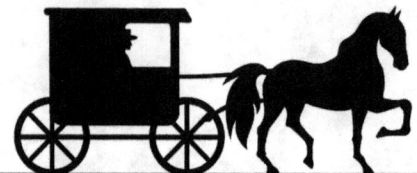

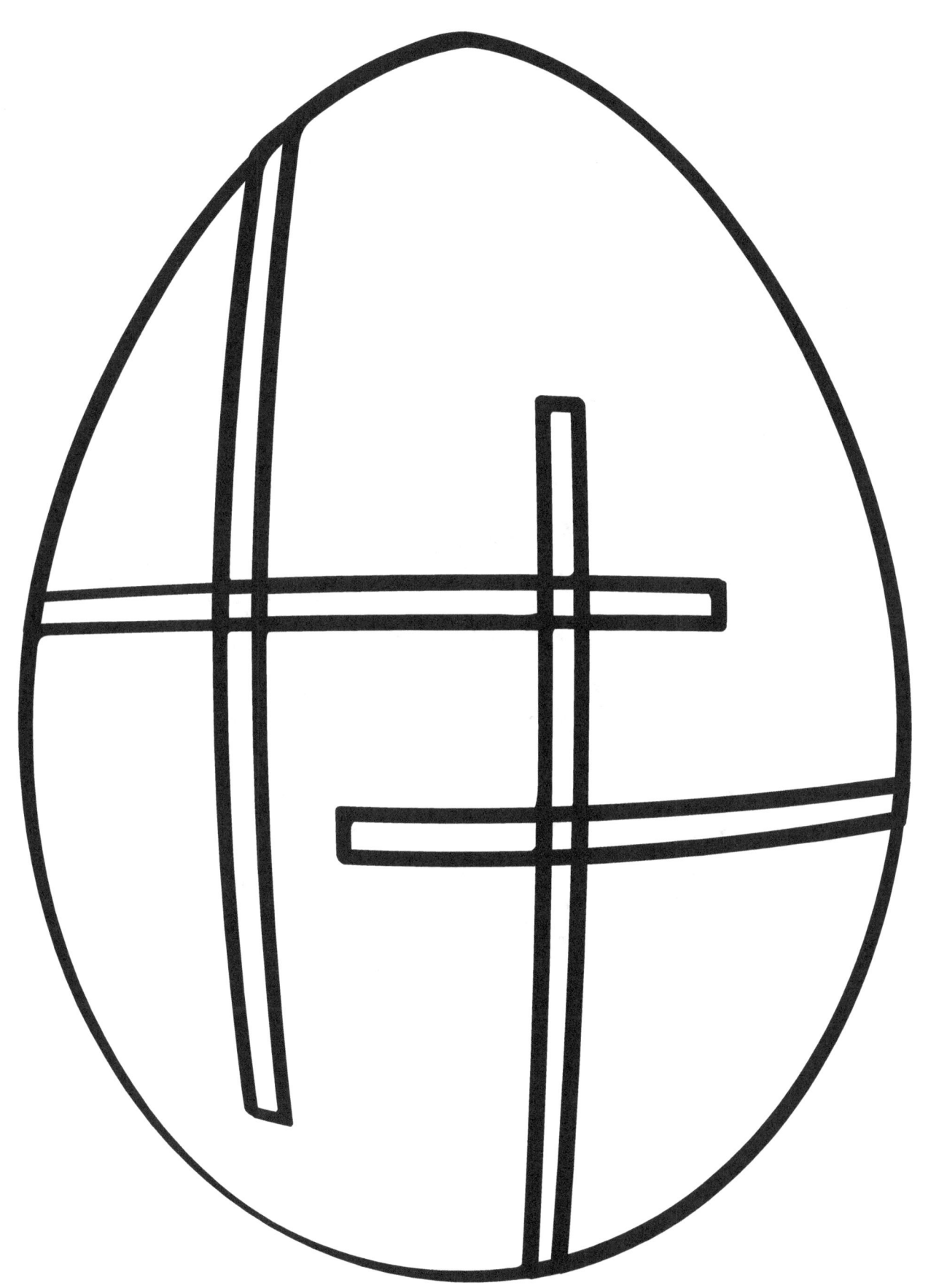

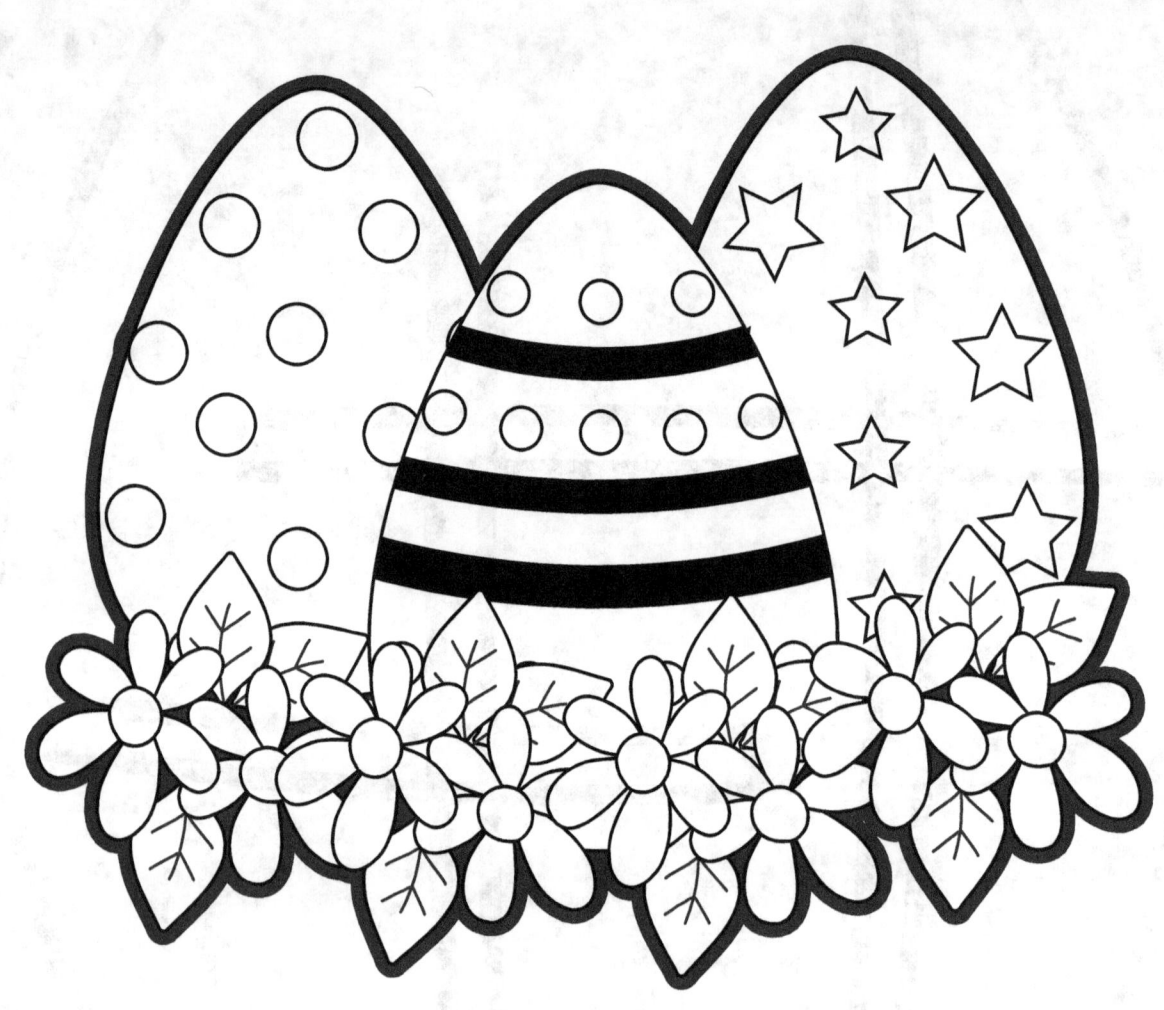

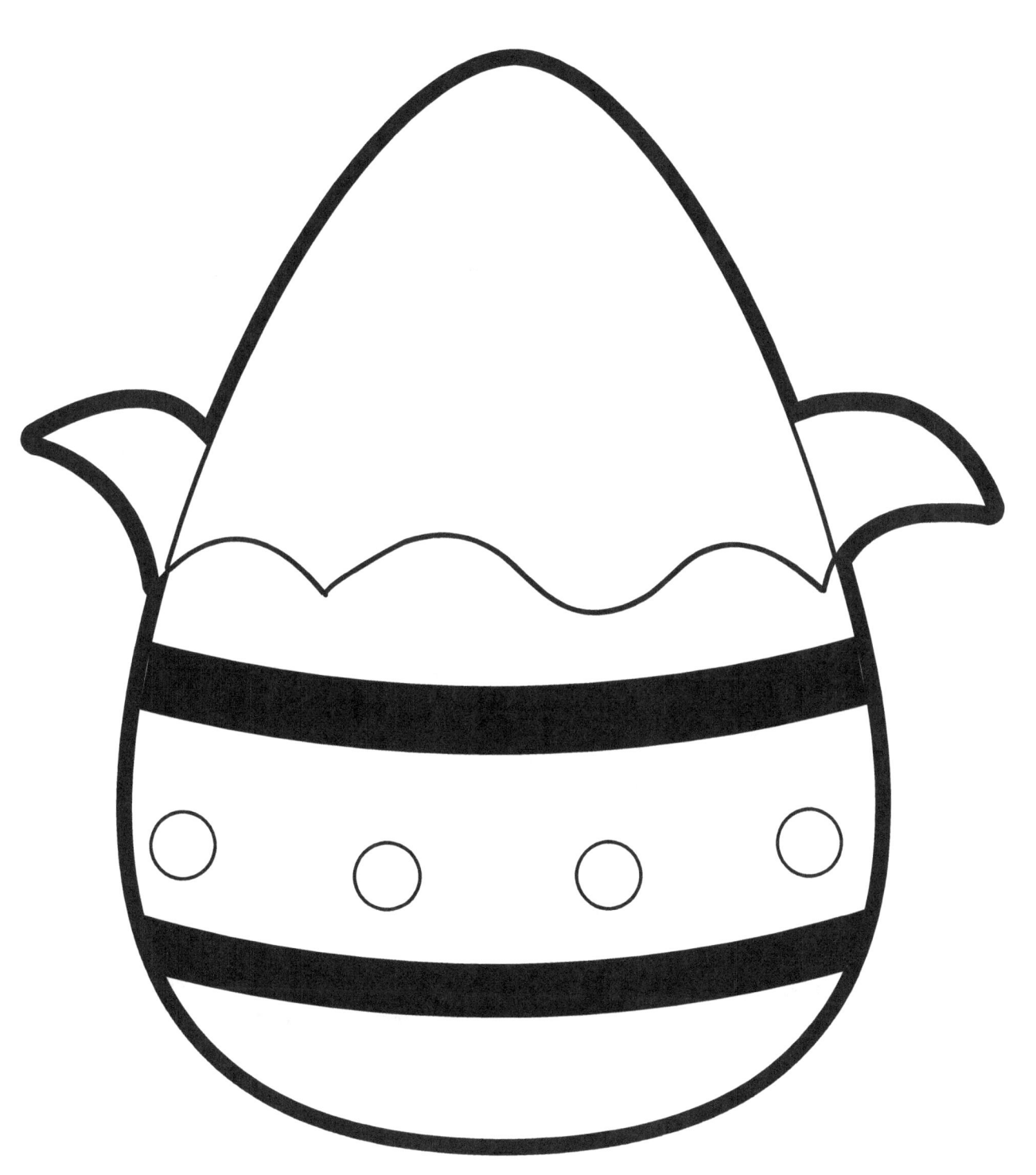

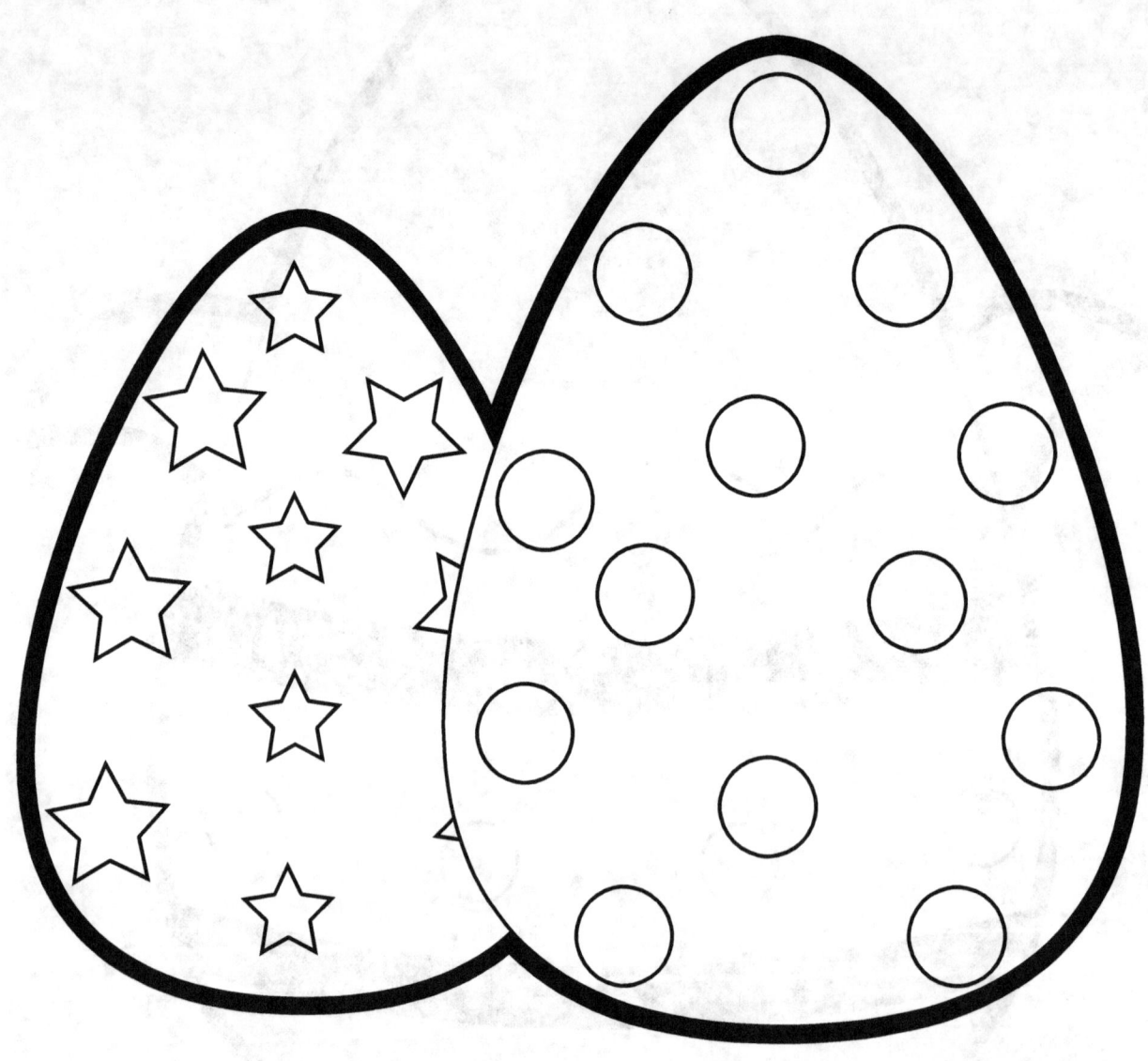

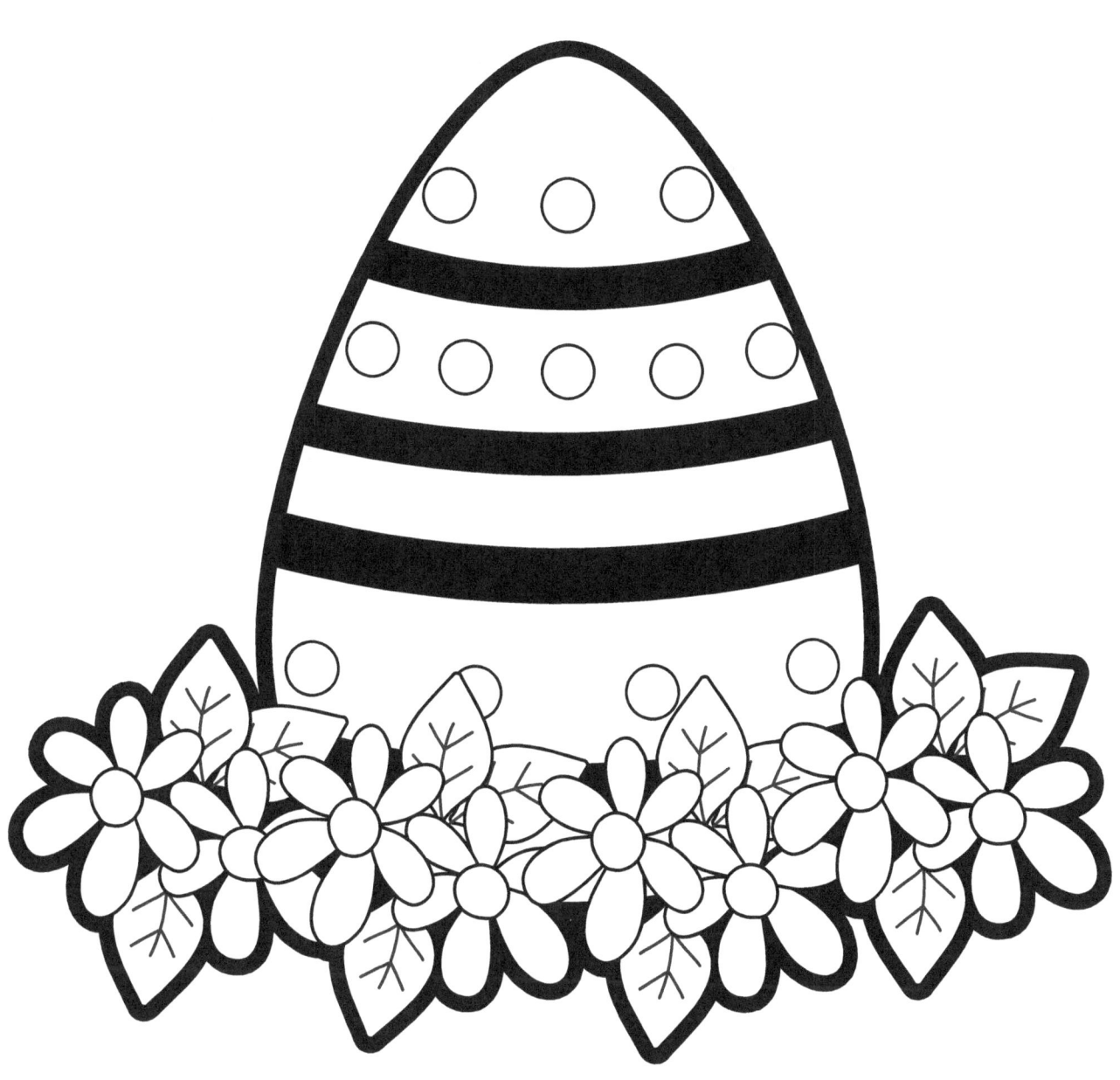

BUNNY

BUNNY

Every year I would sing "Here Comes Peter Cottontail" during Easter for my children. But not all Amish communities are allowed to sing secular songs.

Now that my children are grown, I sing this to my grandchildren while we dye eggs.

WRITING PROMPT: What does a bunny mean to you?

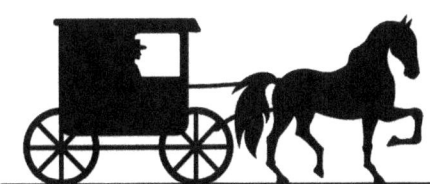

WRITING PROMPT

continued

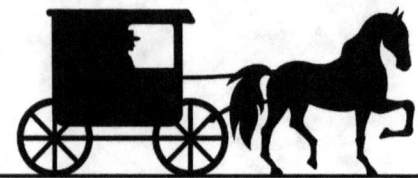

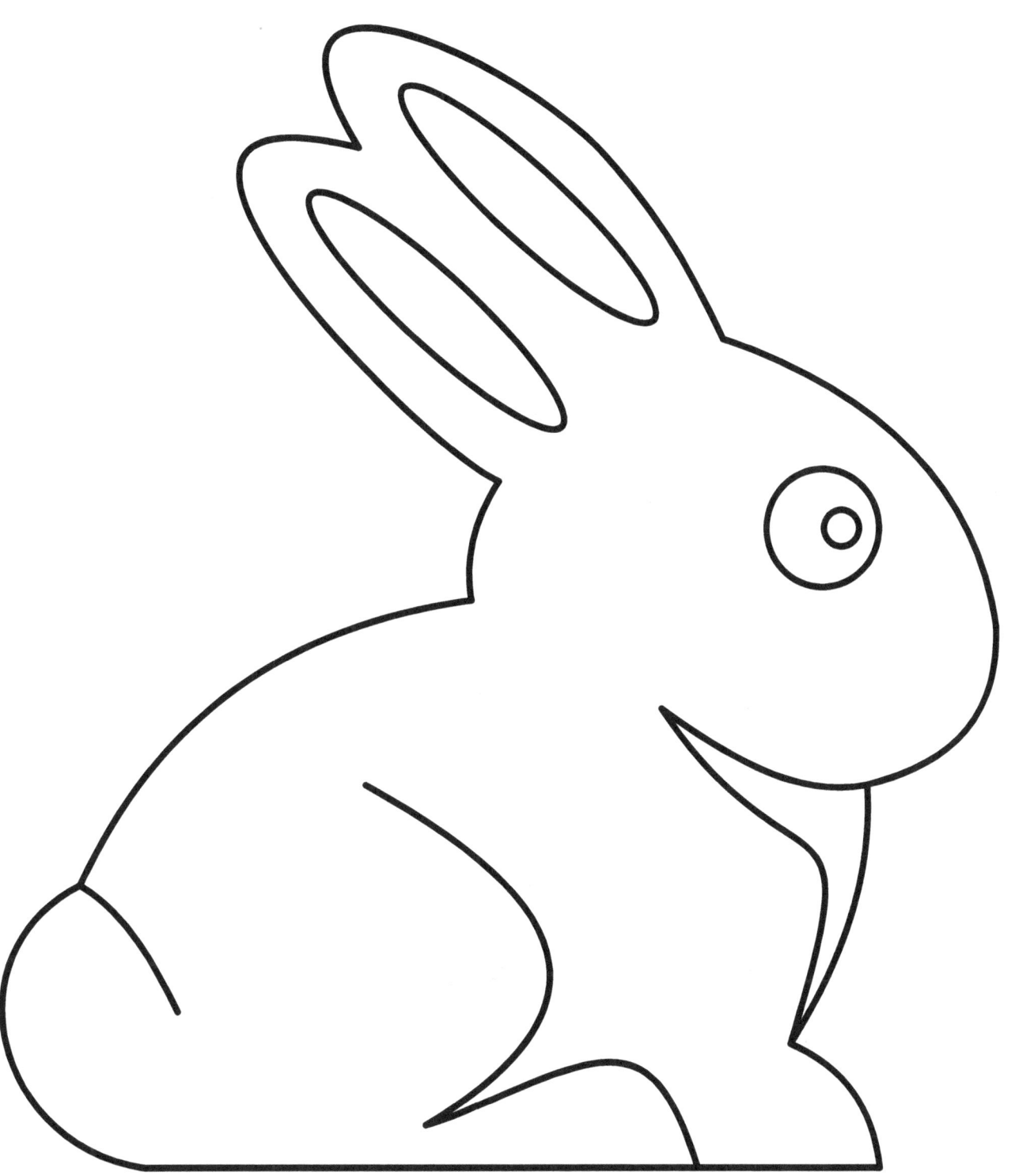

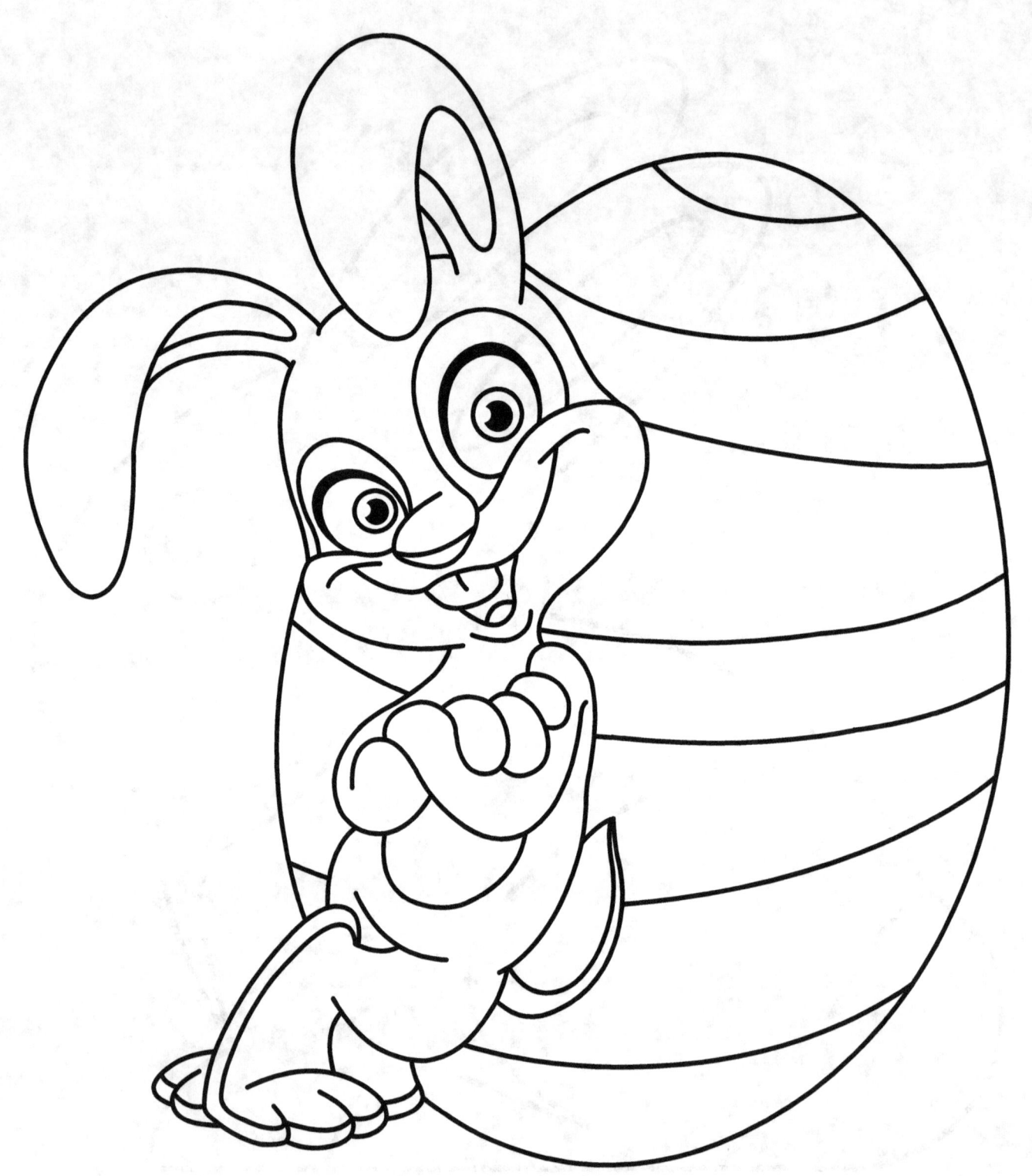

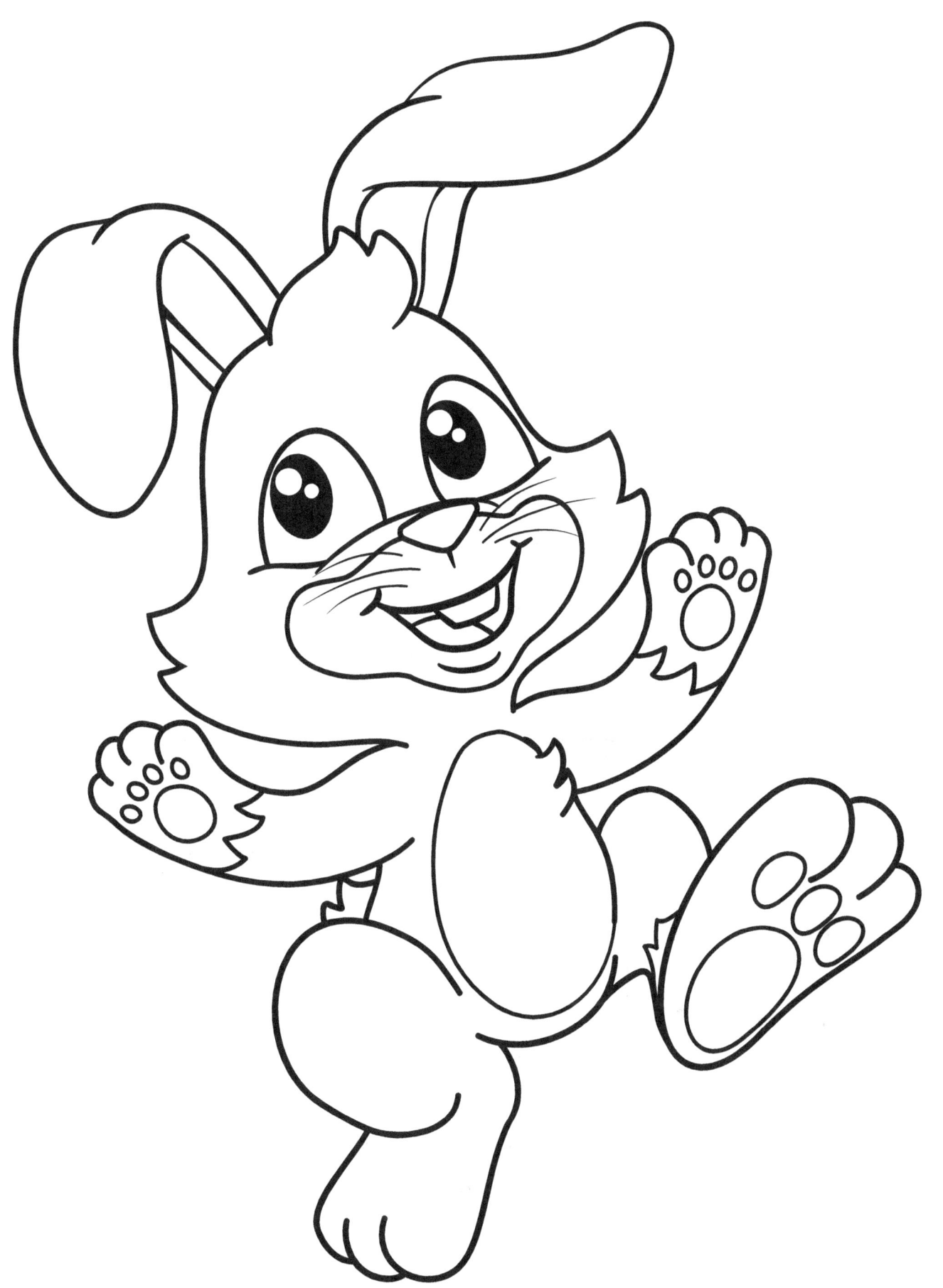

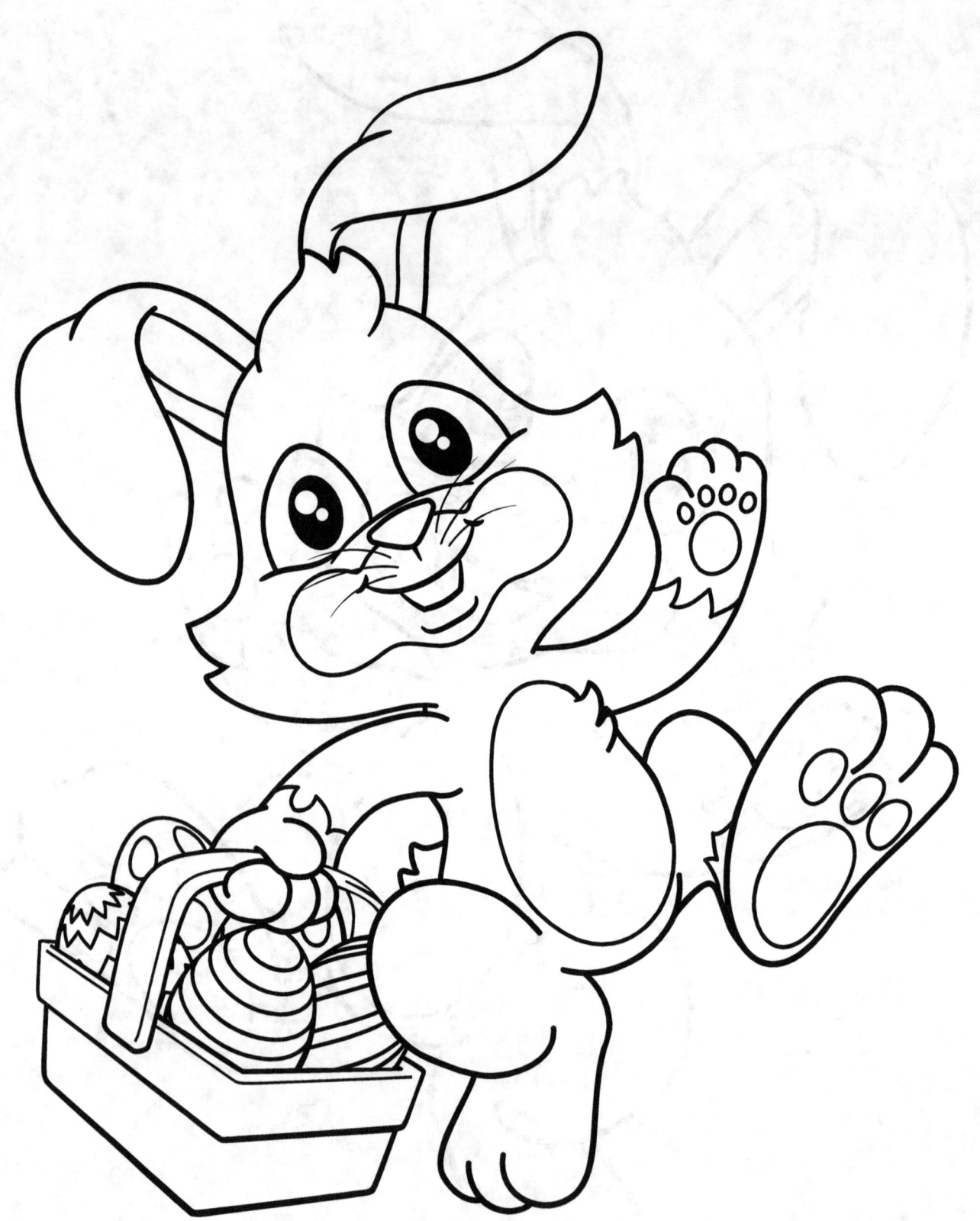

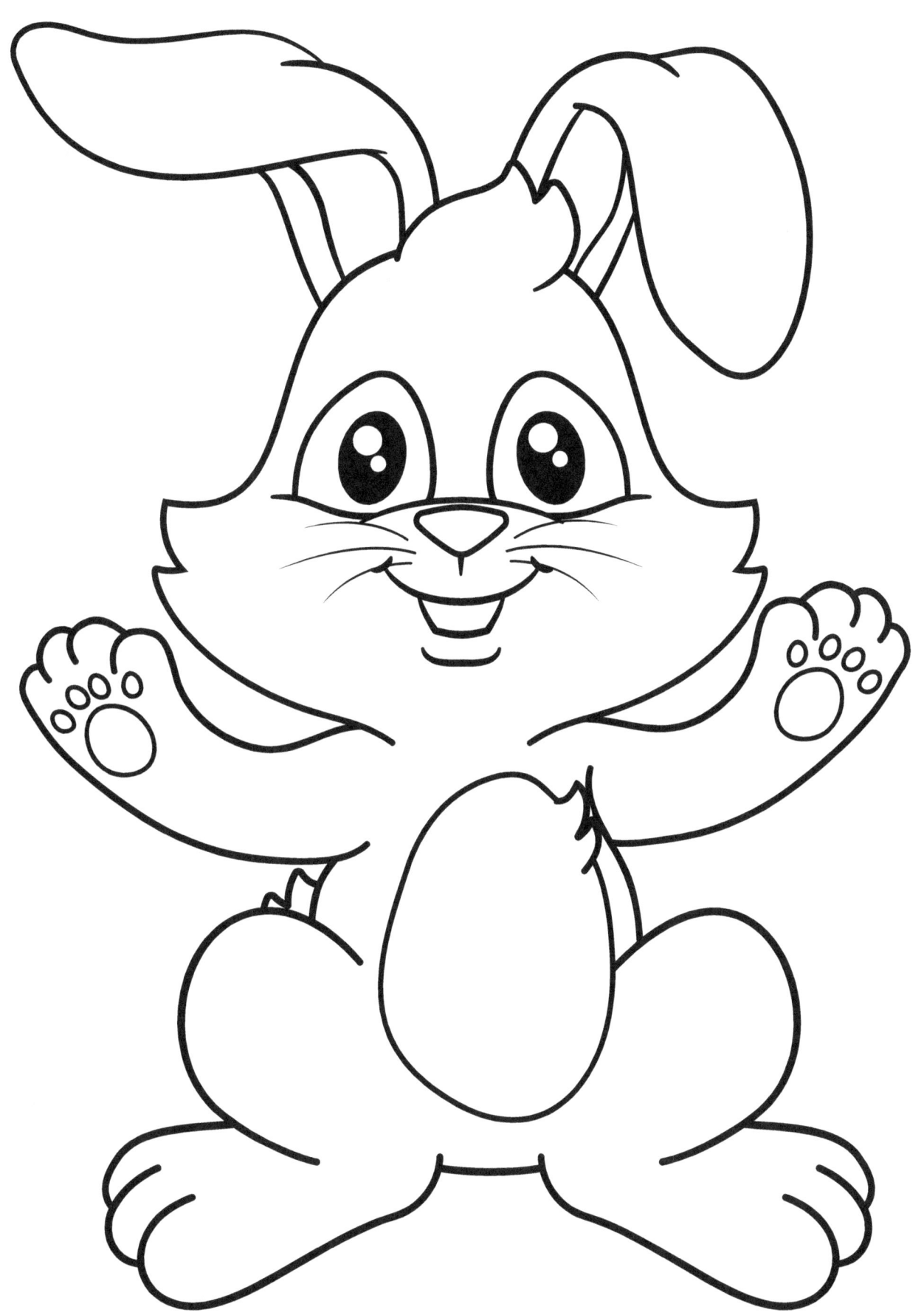

BASKET

BASKET

When I grew up, one of our non-Amish neighbors would stop by every year with an Easter egg basket filled with goodies for us children. I so loved the baskets. They were so pretty!

We children would take turns using the special basket for our egg hunts, the rest of us using a sand bucket or ice cream pail. I have made it a tradition to buy Easter egg baskets for my grandchildren, one for each family. They, too, are taught to share the basket.

WRITING PROMPT: What does a basket mean to you?

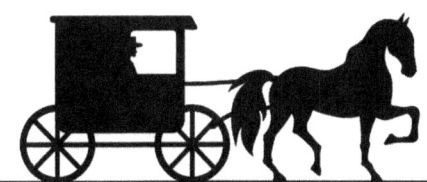

WRITING PROMPT

continued

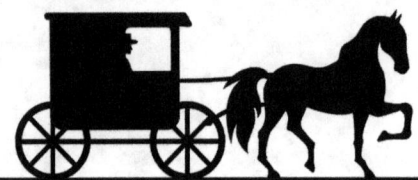

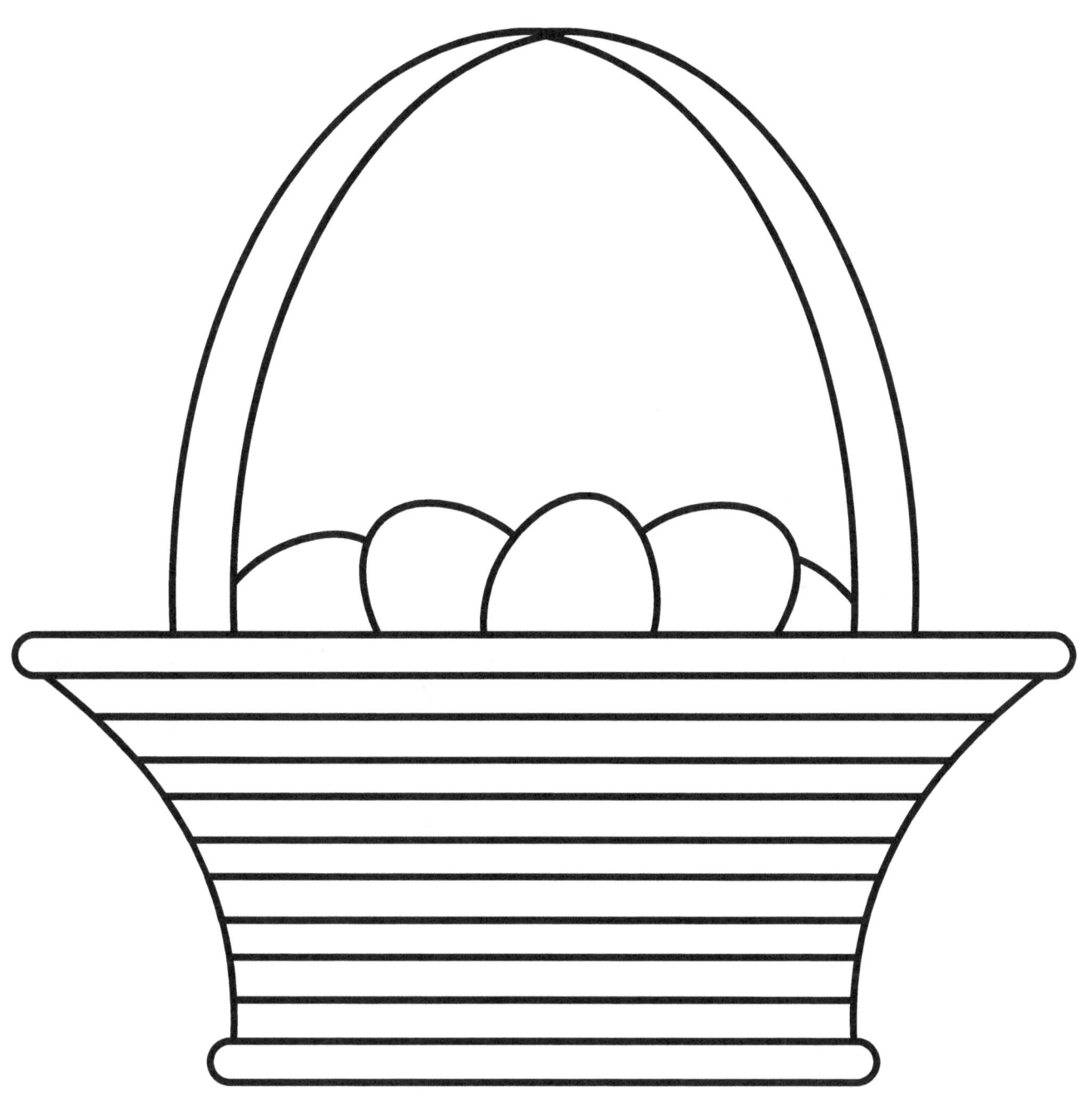

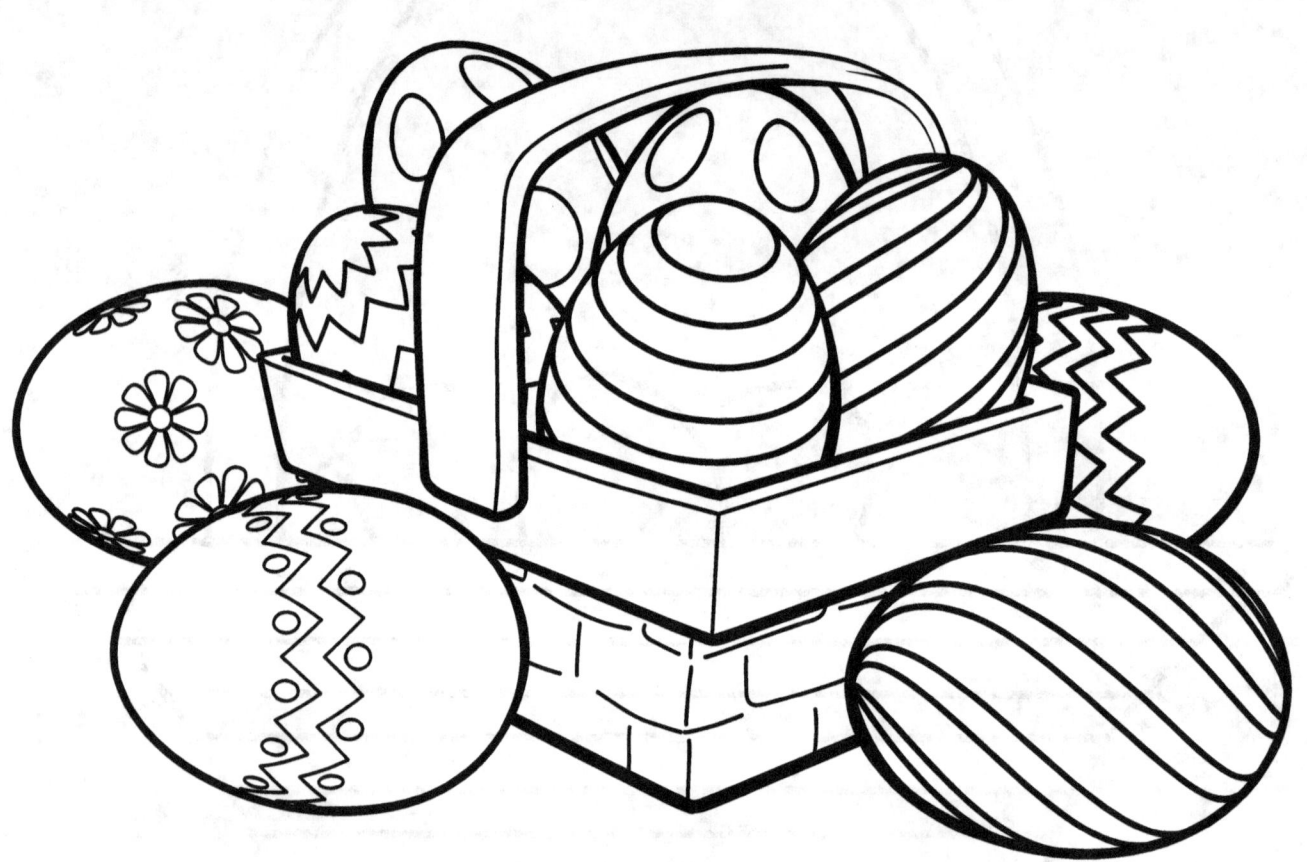

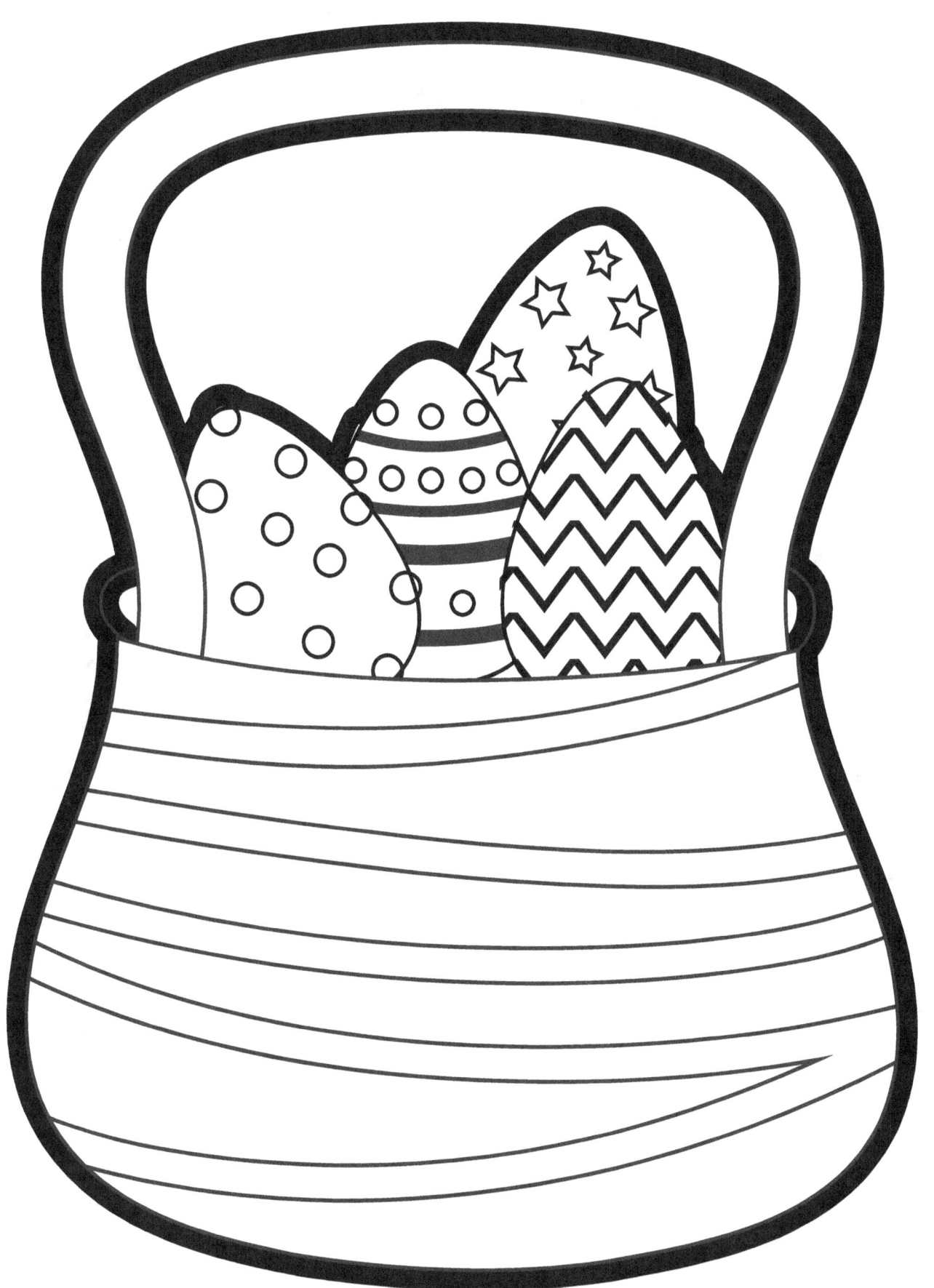

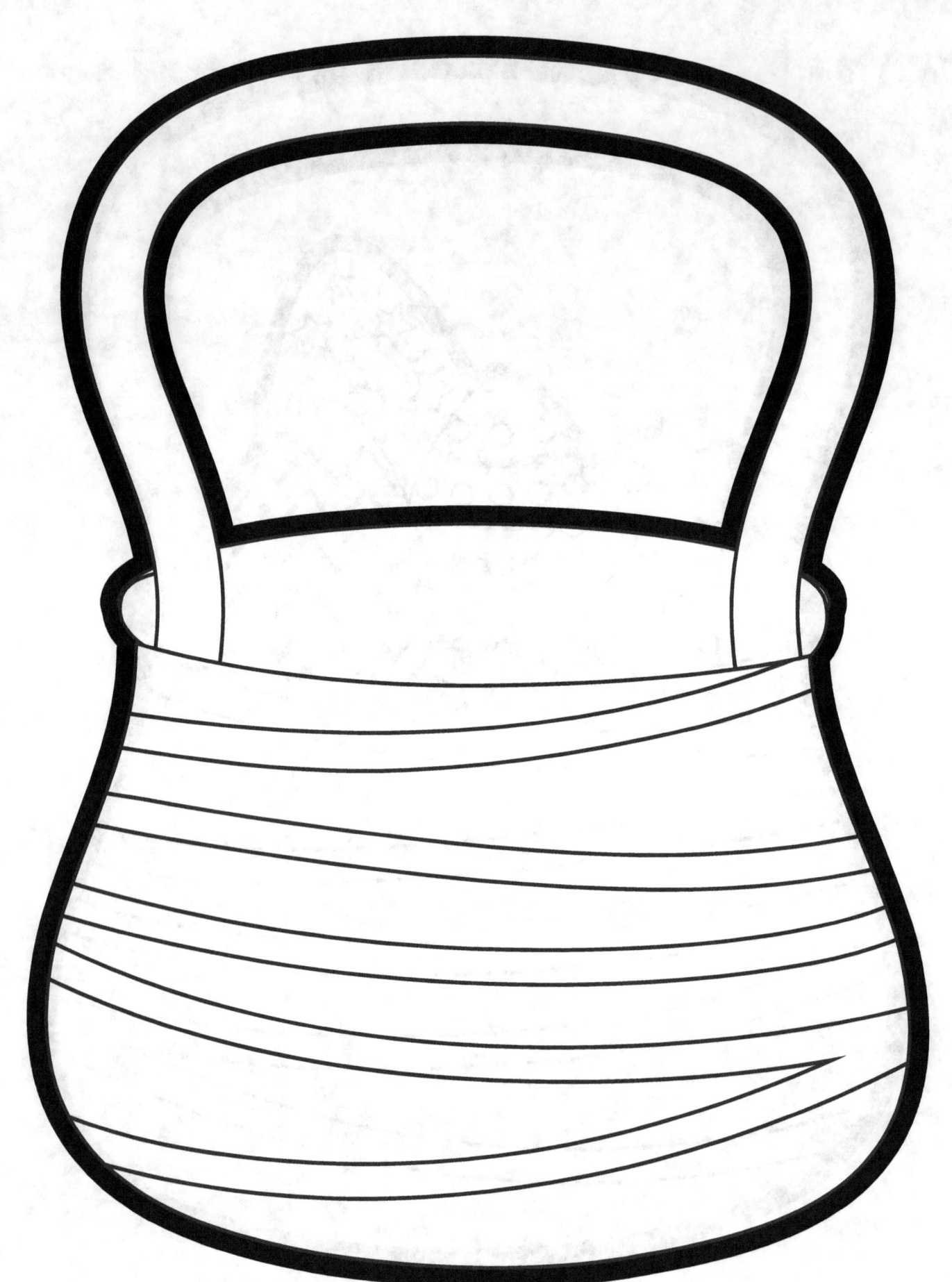

CROSS

CROSS

Crosses are not things you will likely see in traditional Amish homes. Our religion forbids pictures and statues of Jesus, as well as crosses.

But you might find some Amish craftsmen who make wood crosses to sell to non-Amish. And if any of those crosses are in an Amish home, it would most likely only be to serve a useful purpose, such as a coat rack.

WRITING PROMPT: What does a cross mean to you?

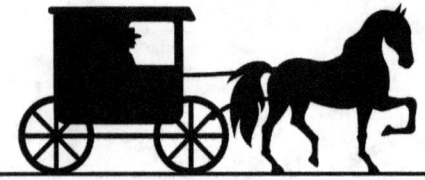

WRITING PROMPT

continued

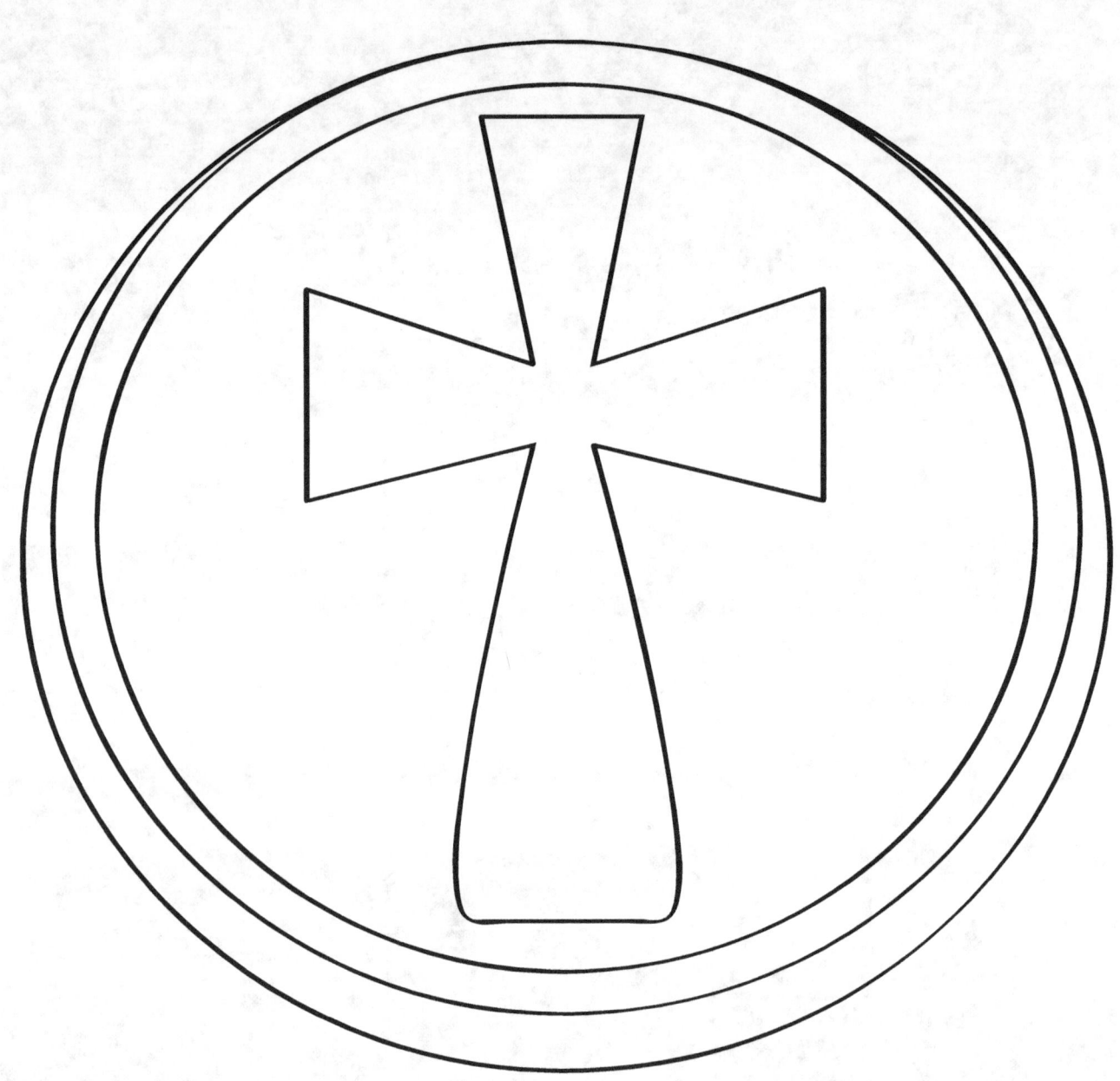

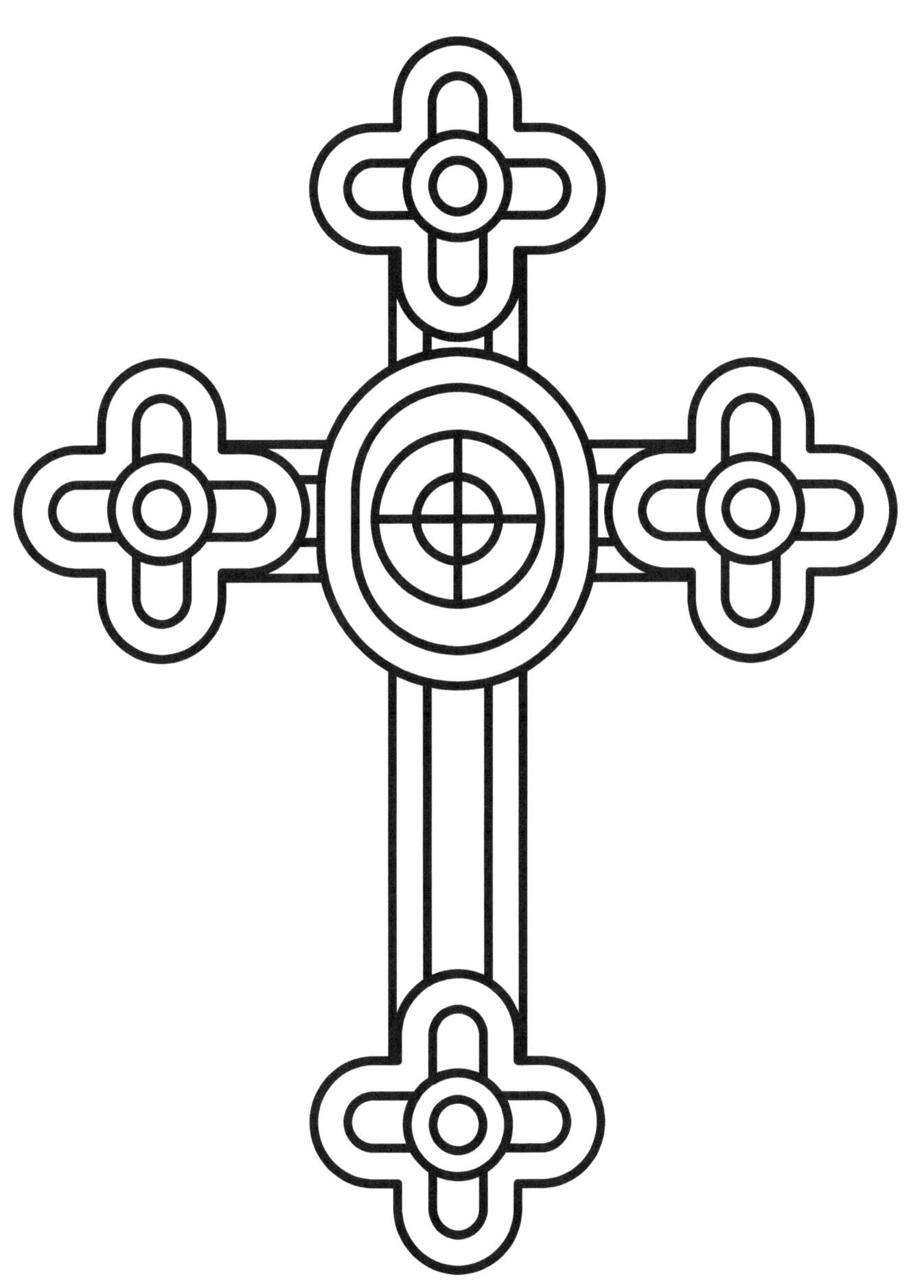

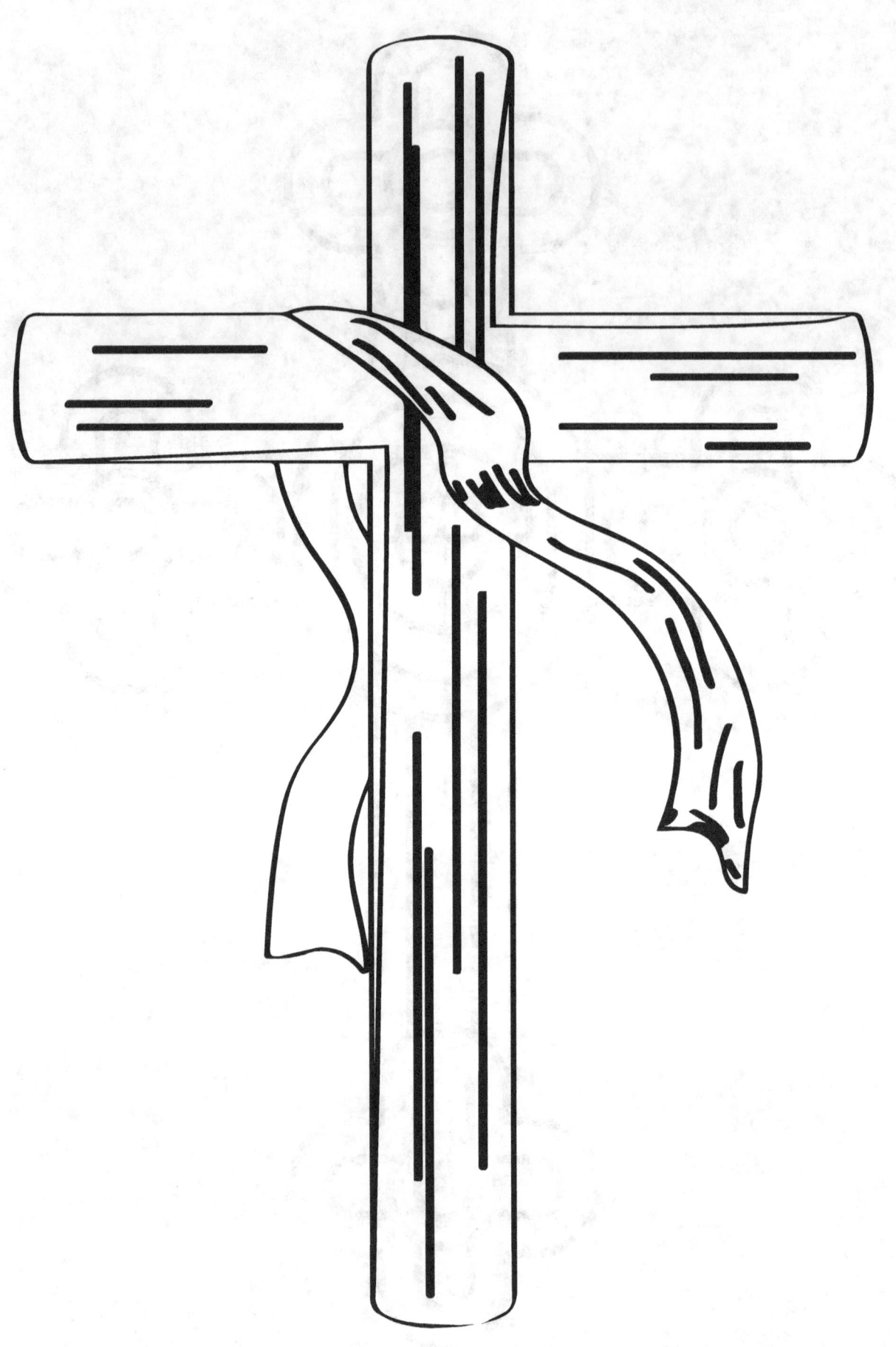

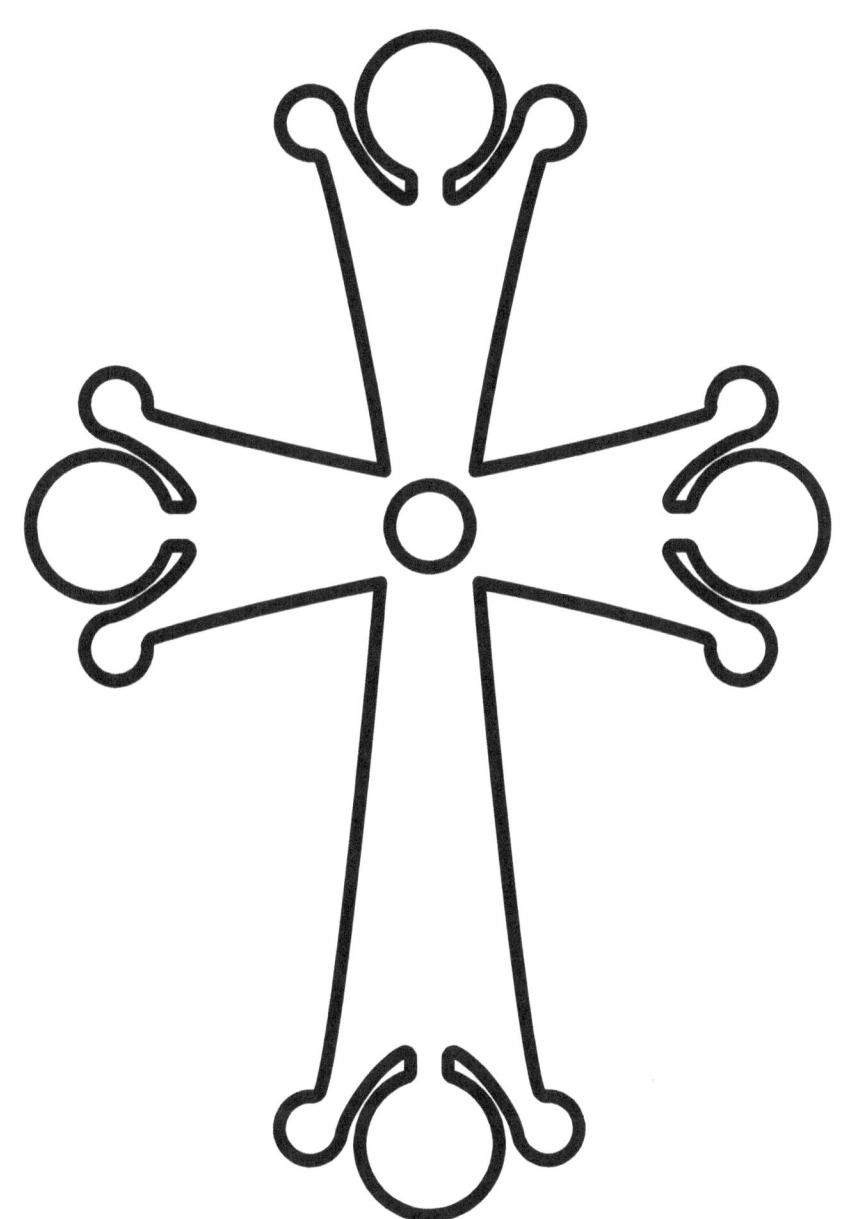

CHICK

CHICK

Every Easter when I was growing up, one of my uncles would treat all of his nieces and nephews to jelly beans on Easter Sunday afternoon when we went over to our grandparents after church.

This is a tradition I have handed down to my children and grandchildren. I also hide yellow Easter marshmallow chicks and chocolate bunnies in the candy bowls full of jelly beans.

WRITING PROMPT: What does a chick mean to you?

WRITING PROMPT

continued

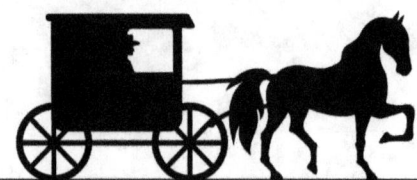

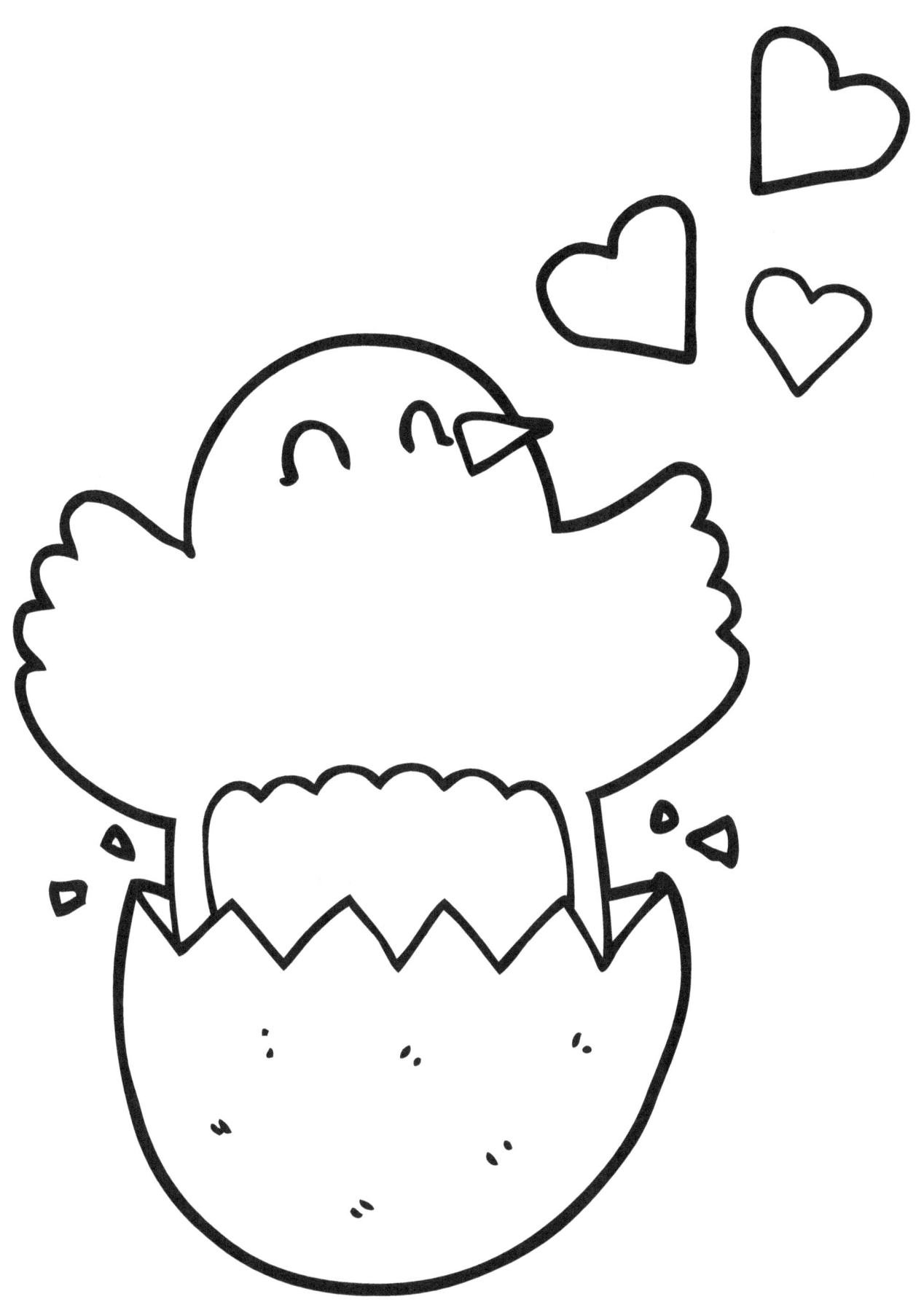

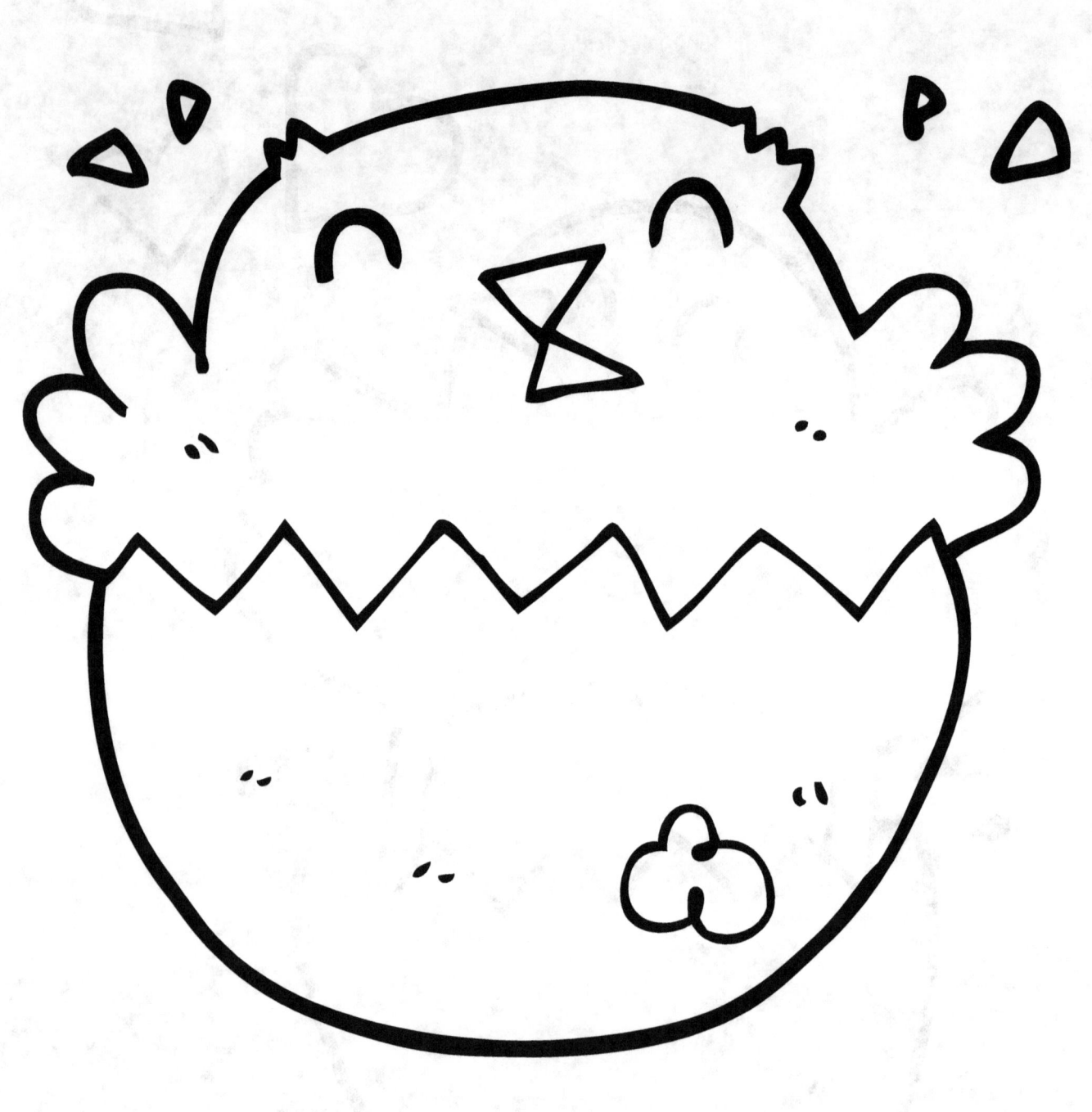

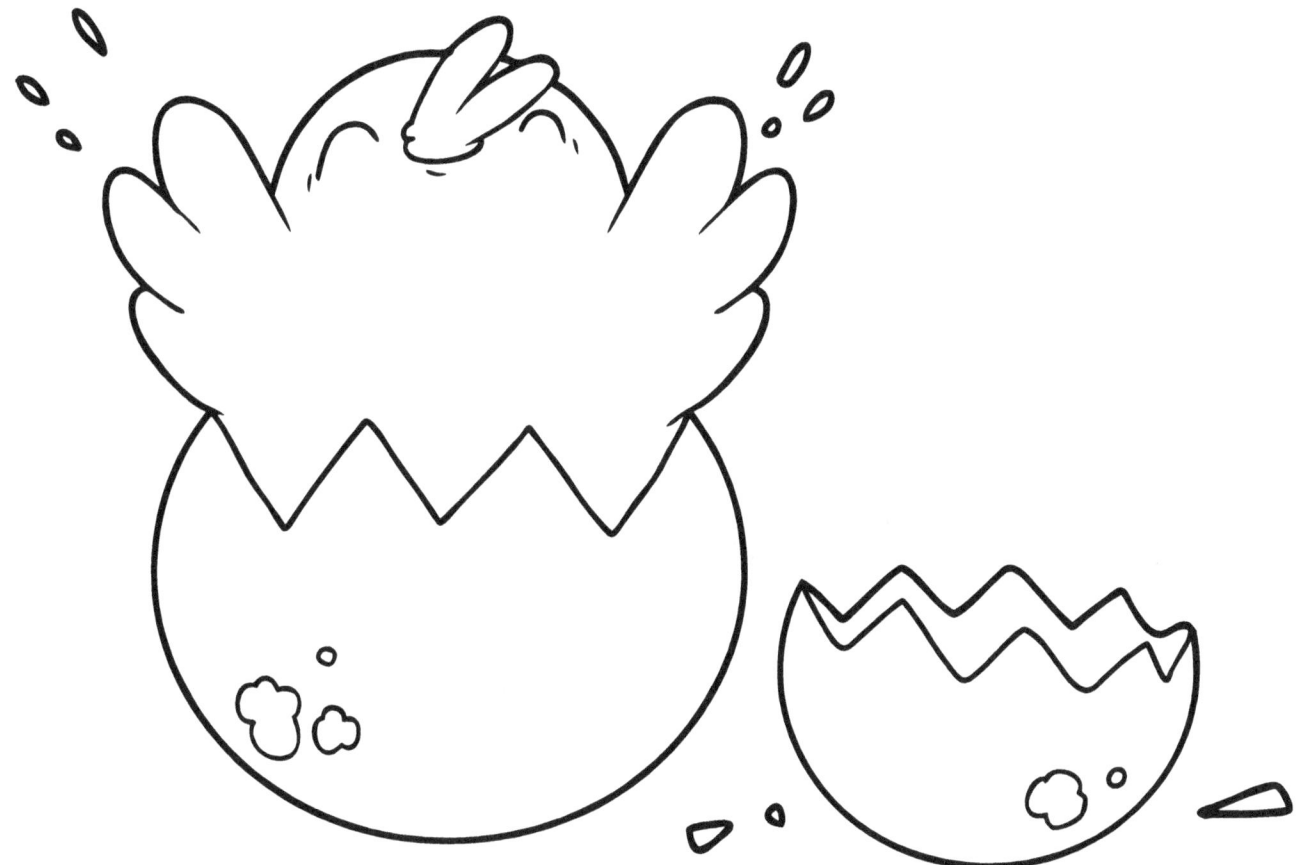

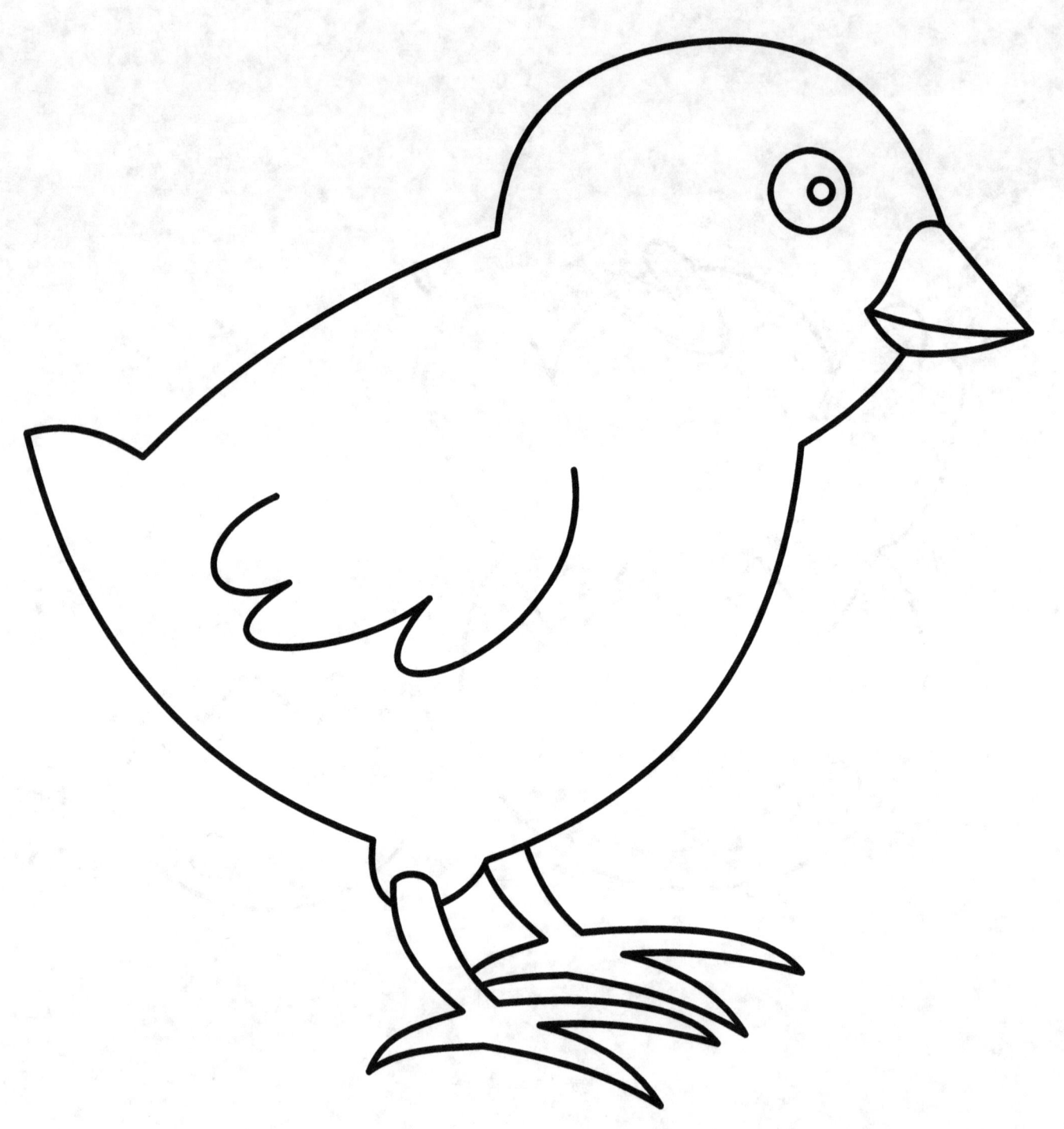

CHURCH

CHURCH

Most people are not aware that we traditional Amish do not have church buildings (with the exception of one or two of the oldest communities). We have services in our homes.

We attend church every other Sunday and we do not have services on Easter Day, unless it falls on the Sunday when we normally go to church. We hear about Good Friday and Jesus' resurrection on the Sundays before Easter, if we do not attend church that day.

WRITING PROMPT: What does a church mean to you?

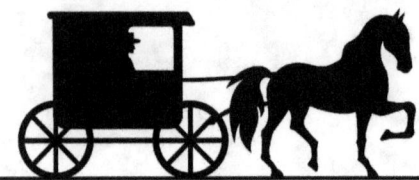

WRITING PROMPT

continued

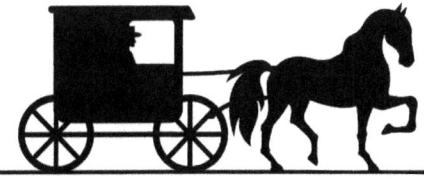

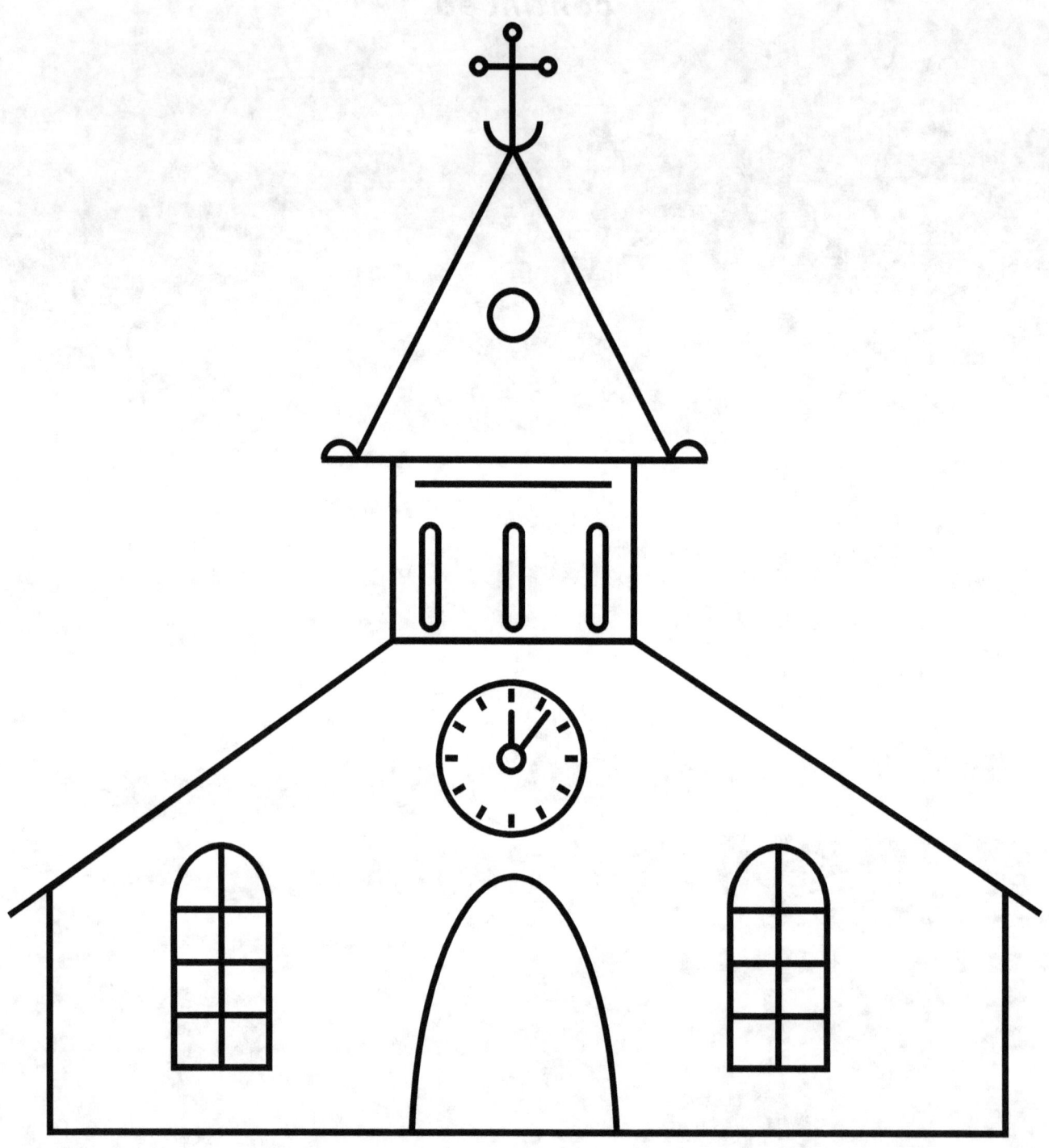

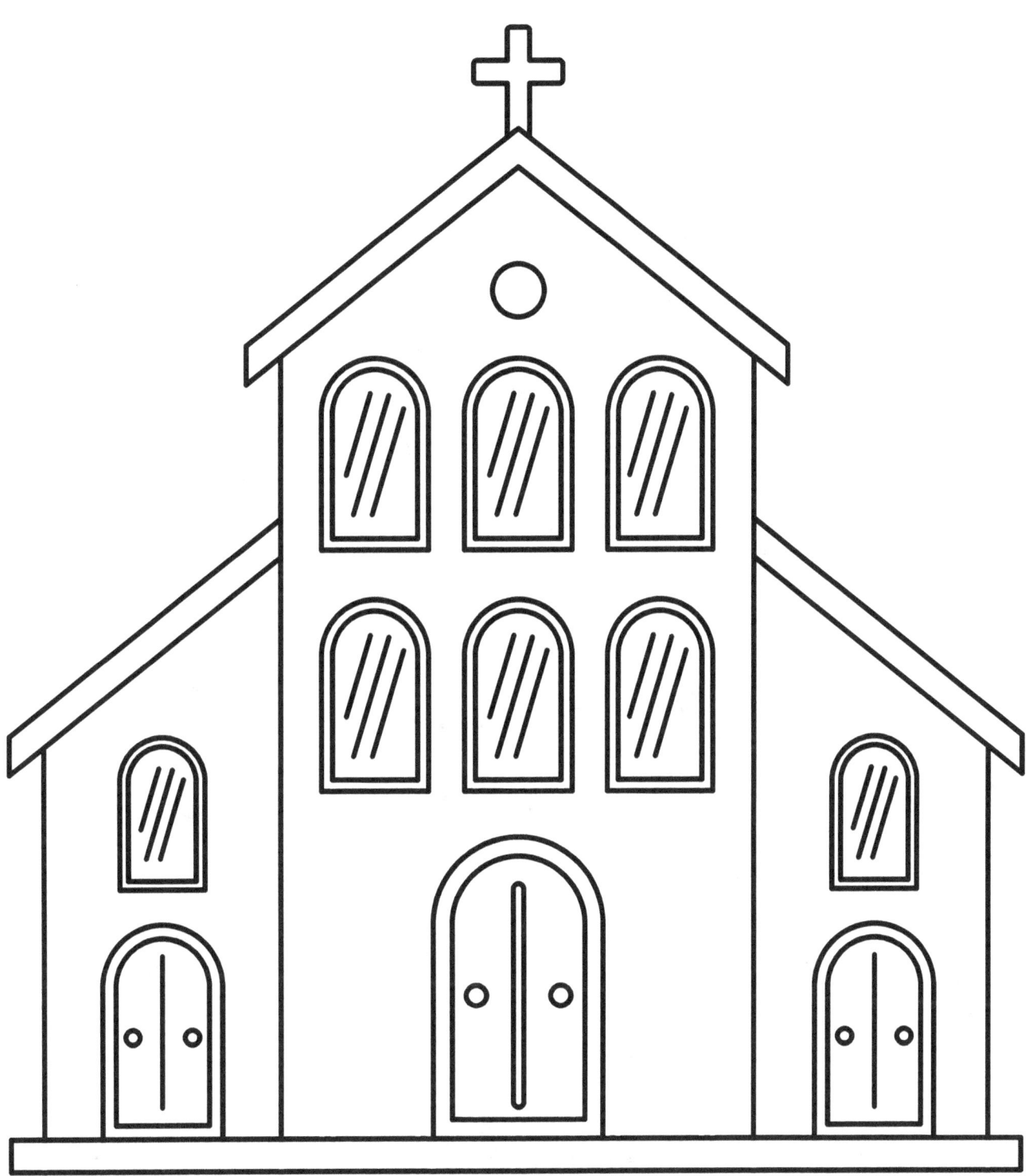

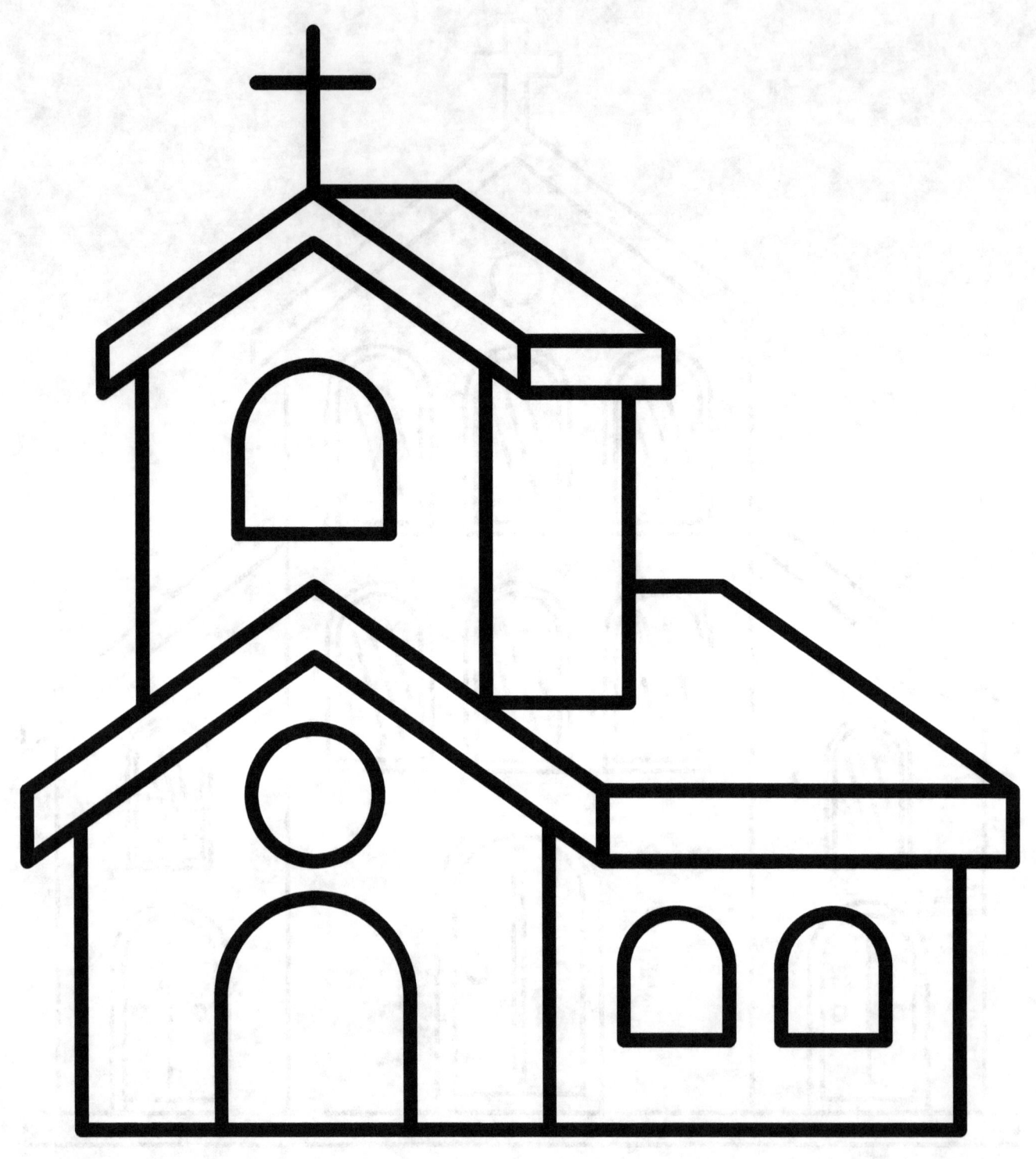

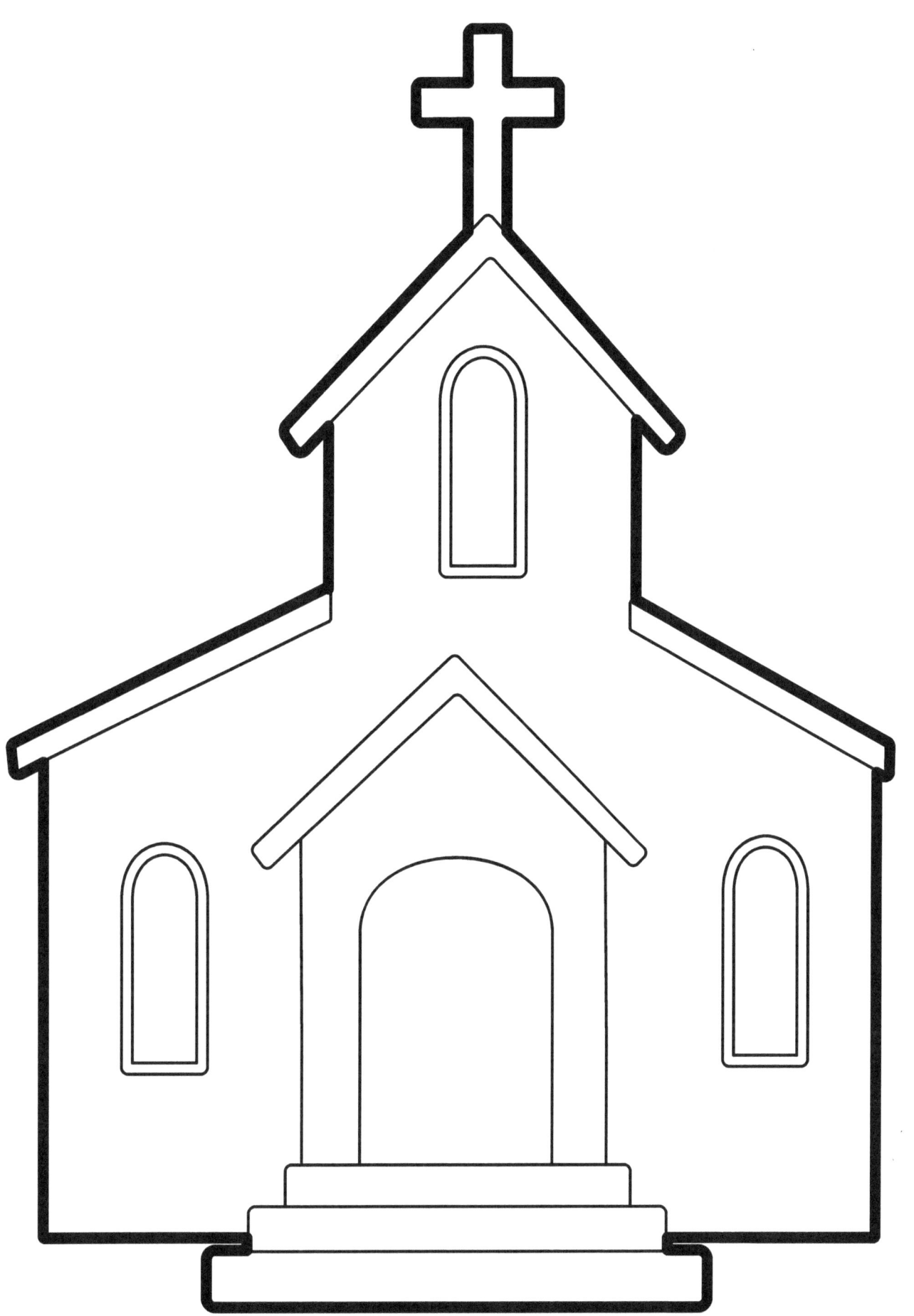

TULIP

TULIP

To me, tulips are part of Easter. Seeing the tulips bloom remind me of Jesus' resurrection. They are also a sign that the long dark winter is over and God is blessing us with another year of planting, gardening, and eventually, harvest.

My children know how much tulips mean to me, so every Easter they bring bouquets of tulips to Easter dinner at our house.

WRITING PROMPT: What does a tulip mean to you?

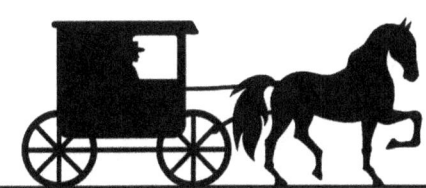

WRITING PROMPT

continued

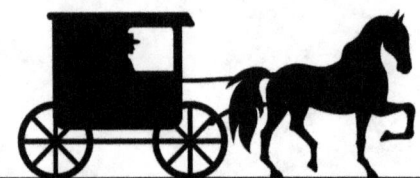

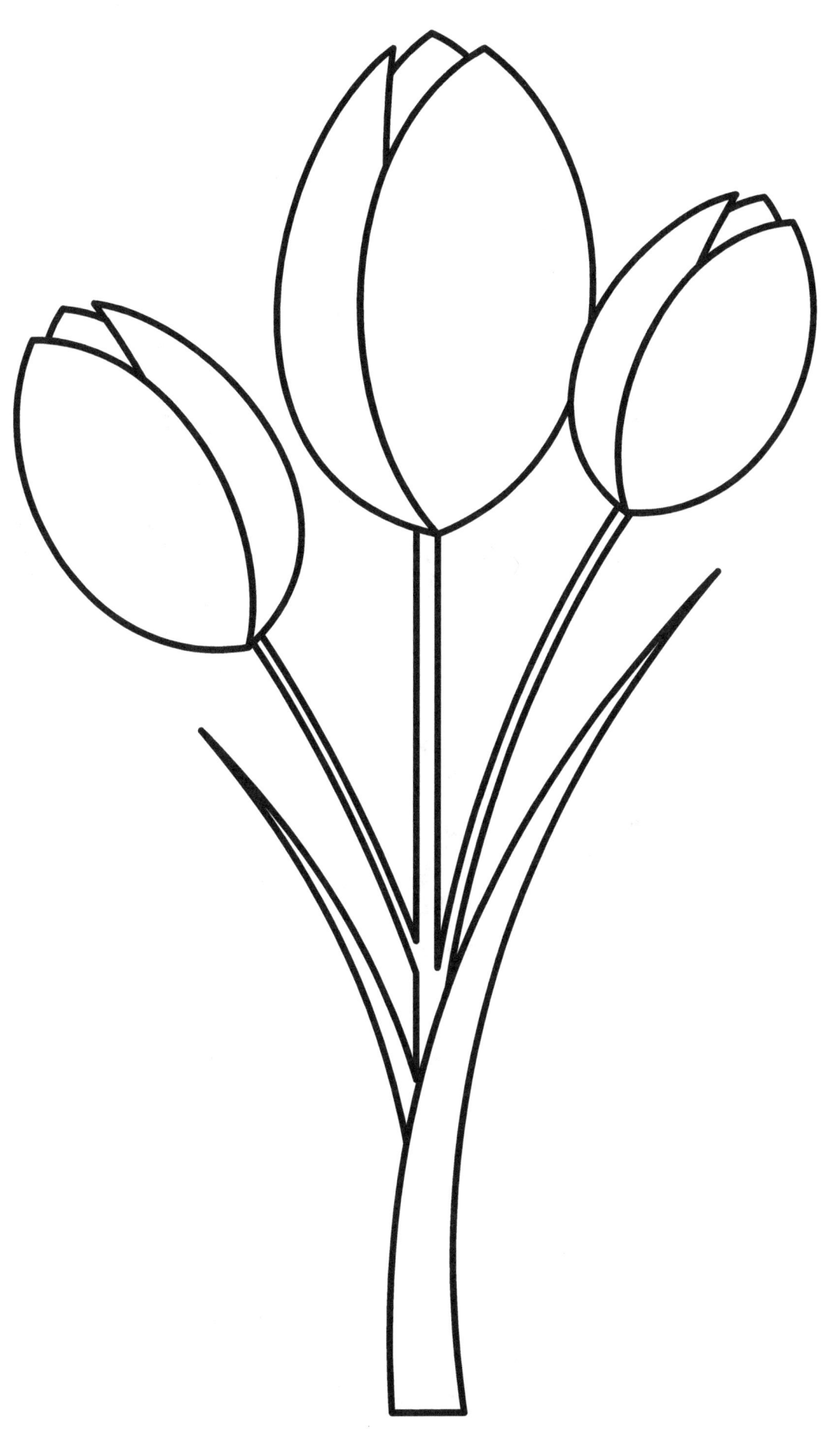

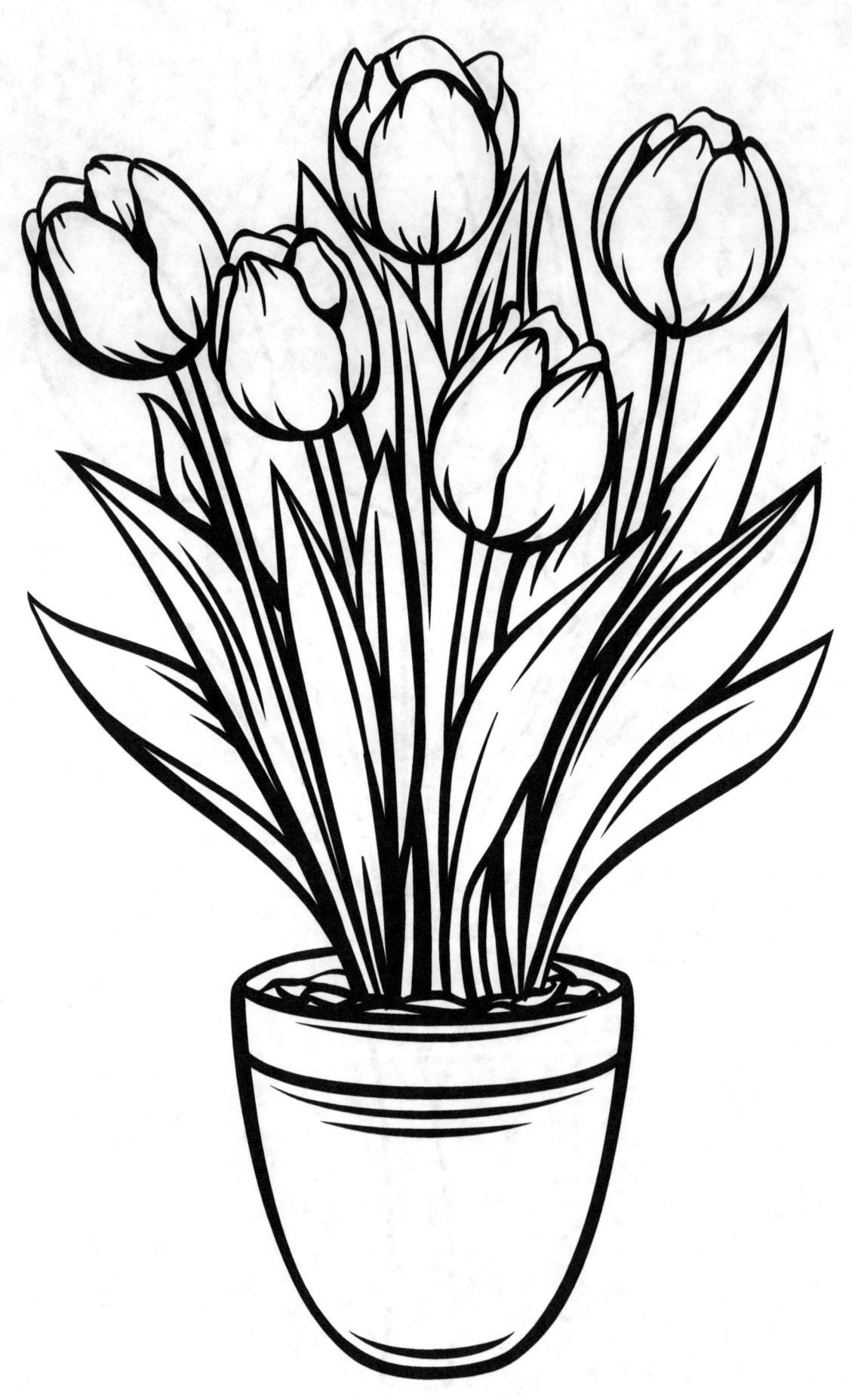

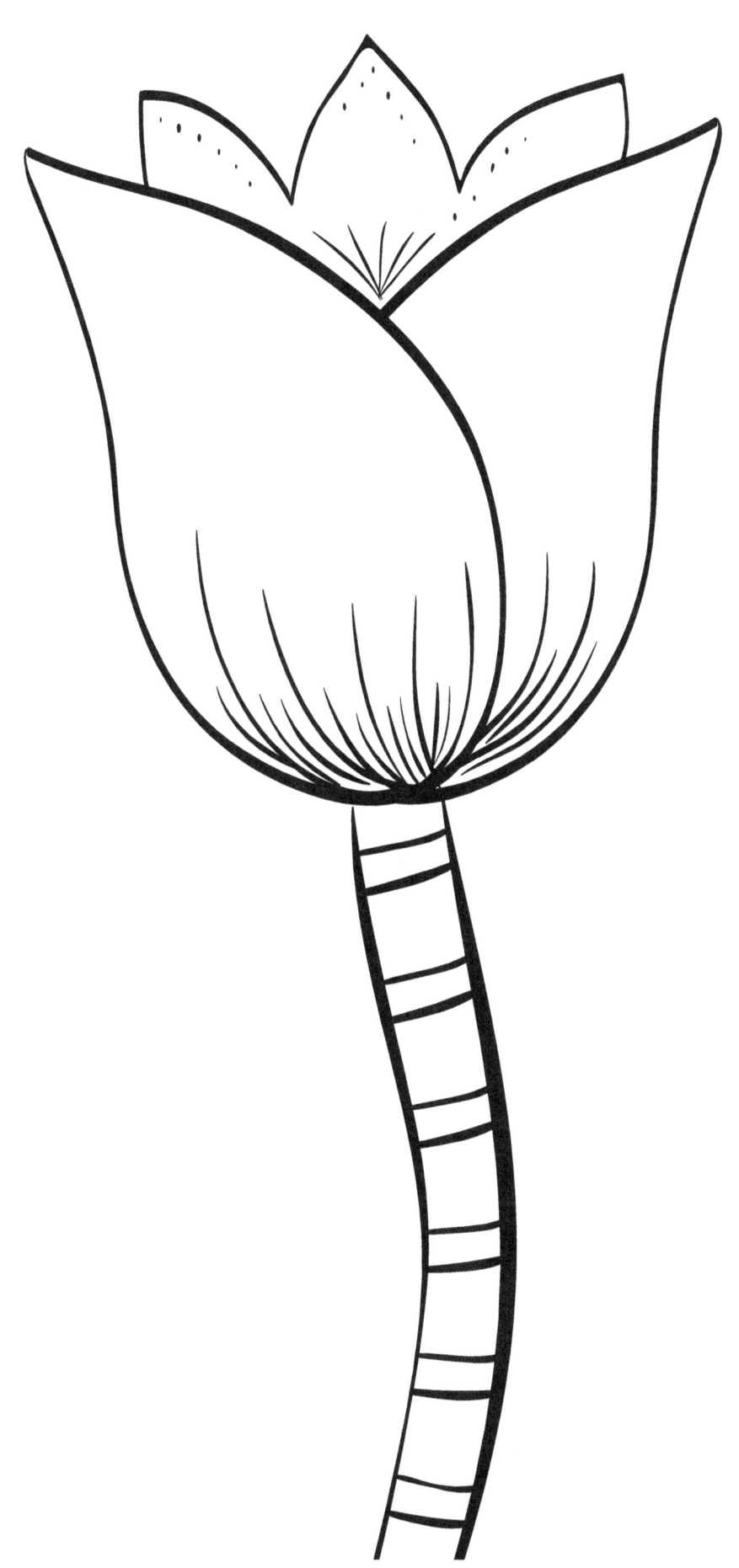

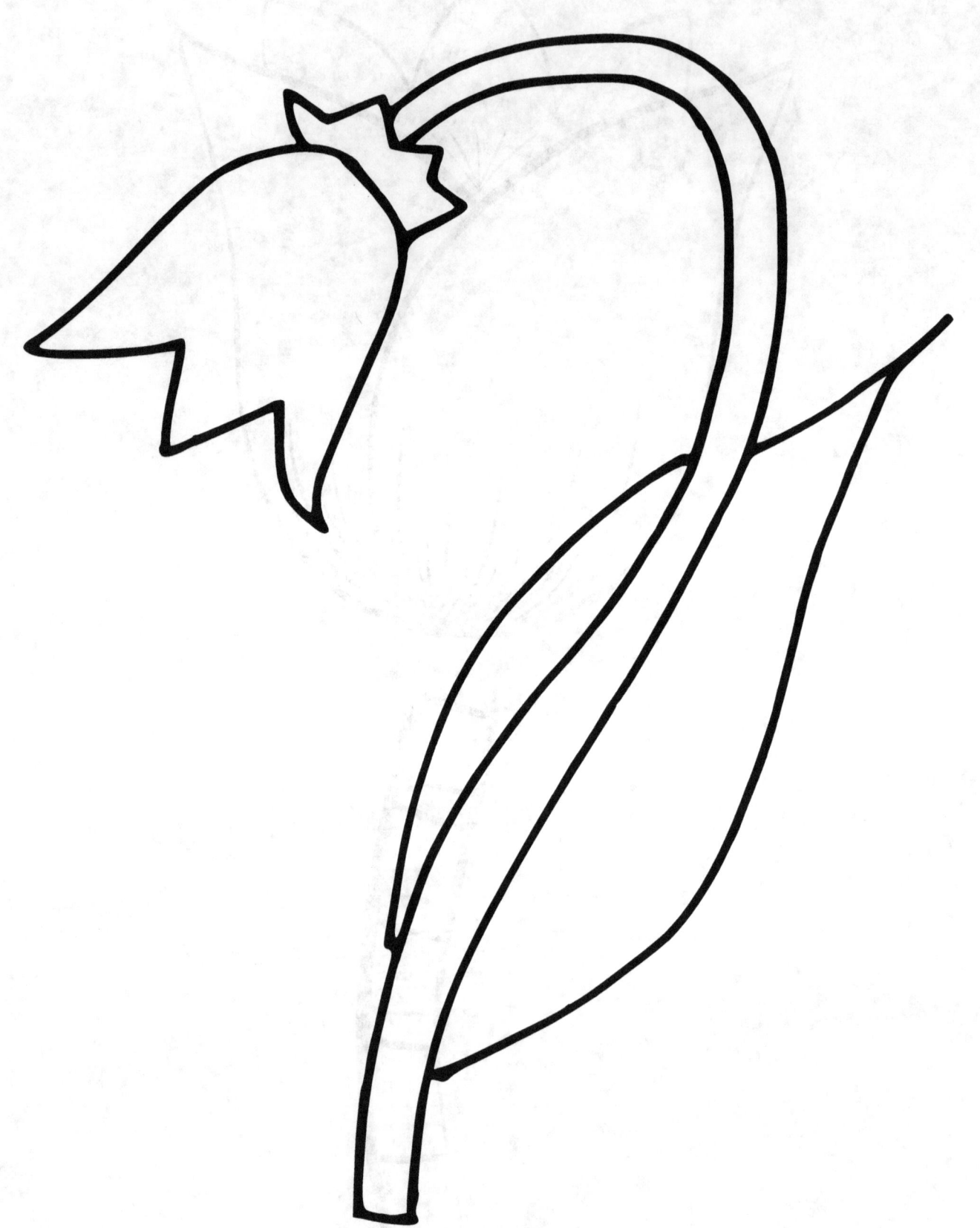

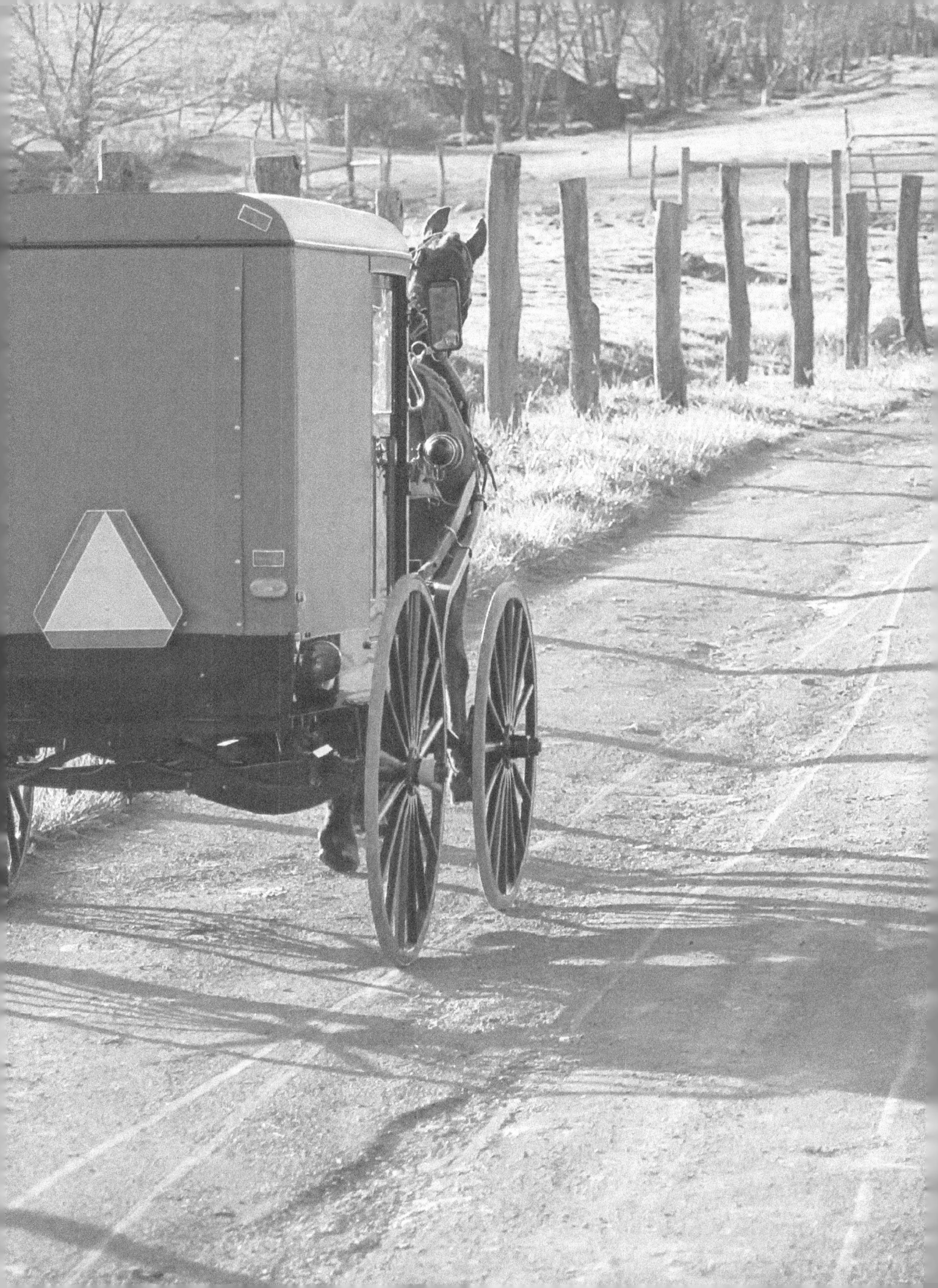

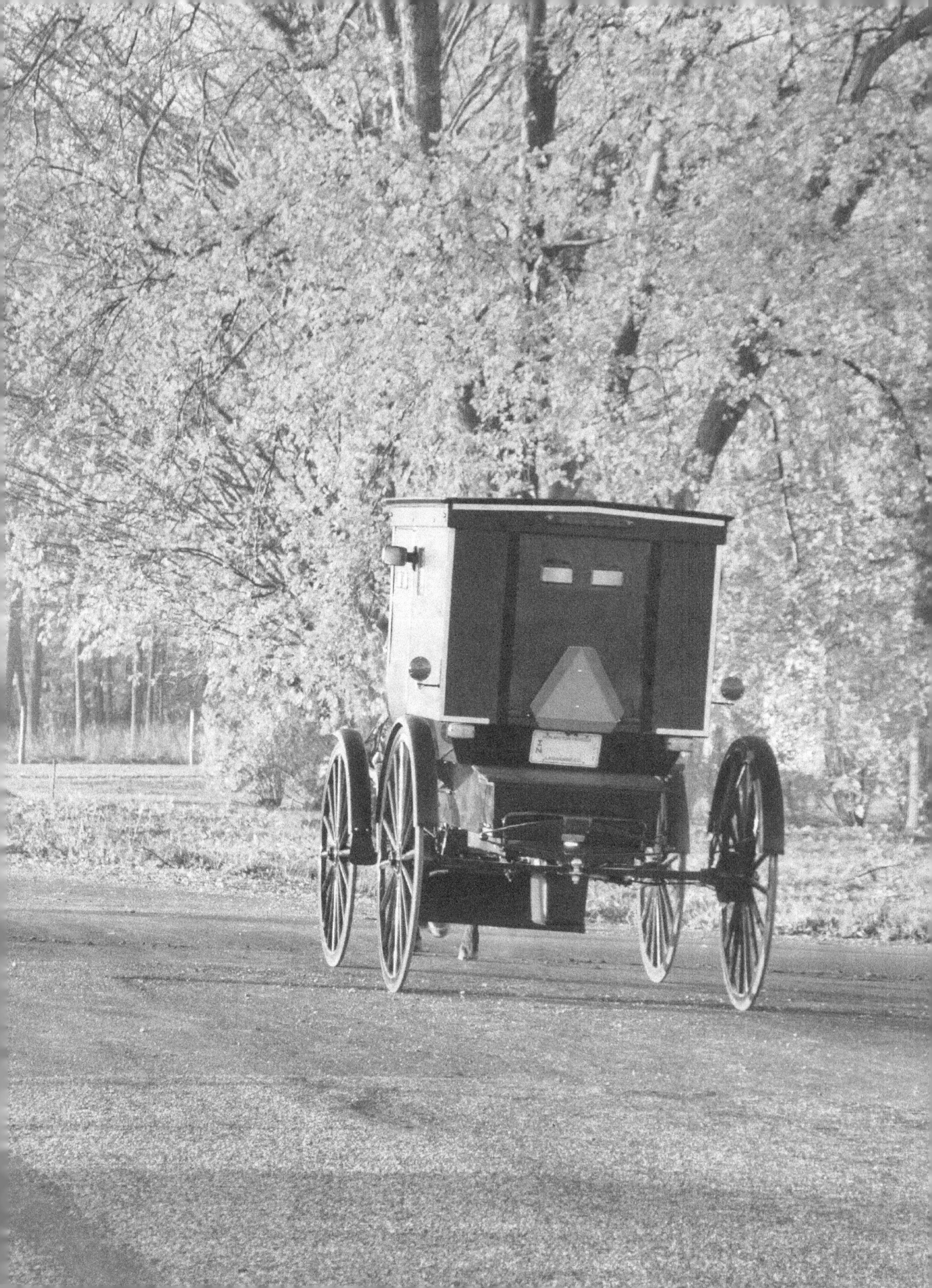

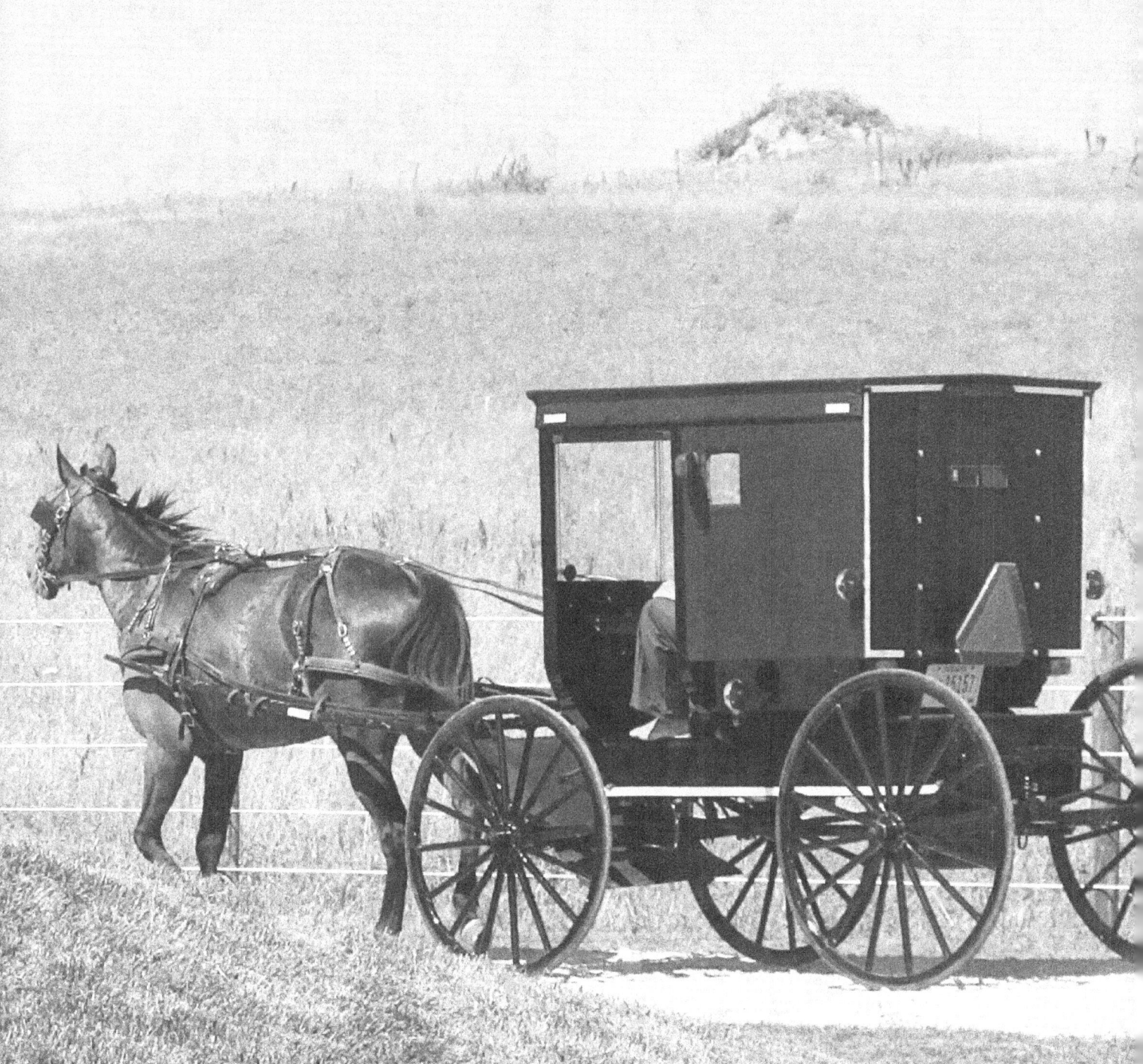

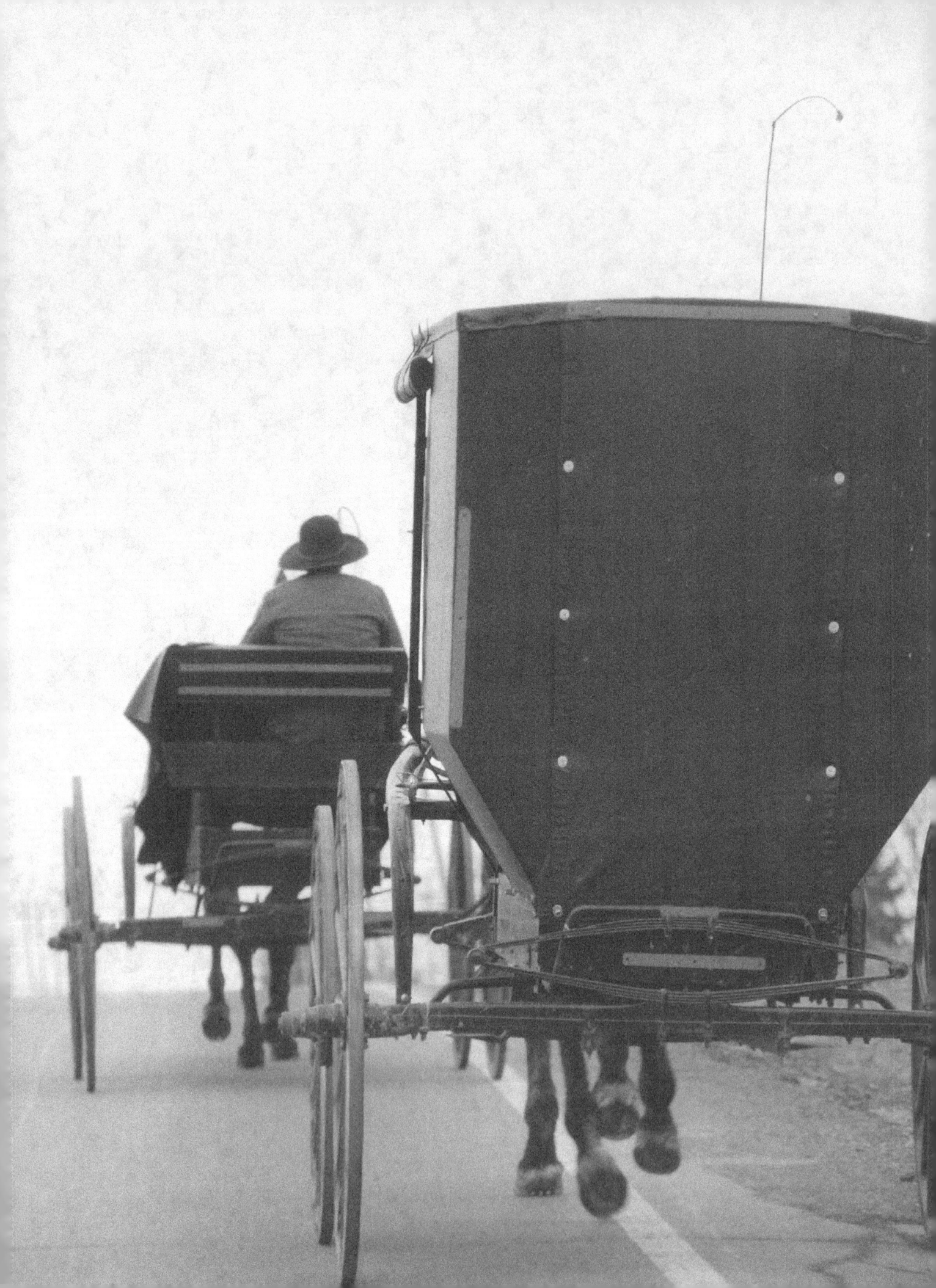

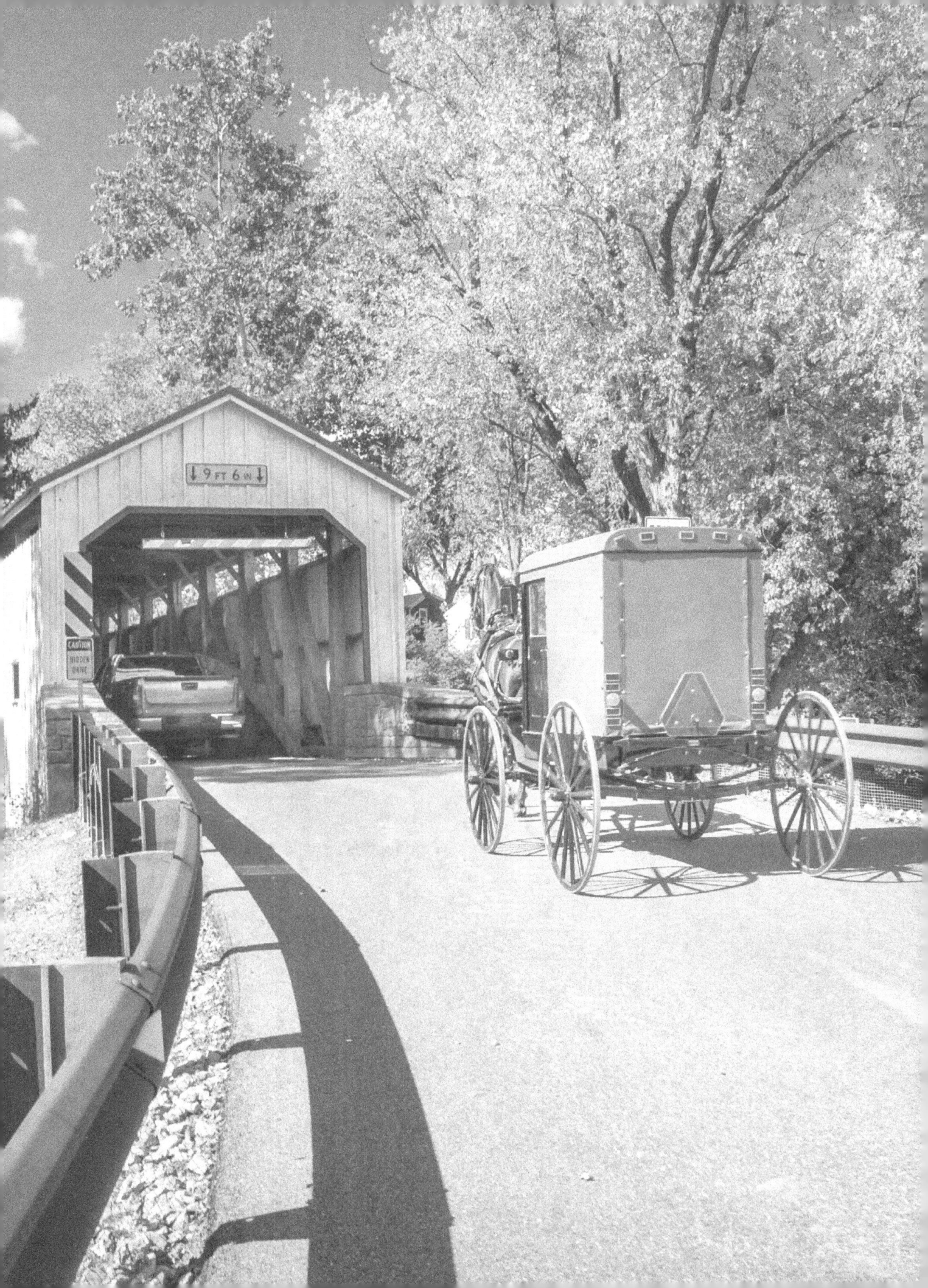

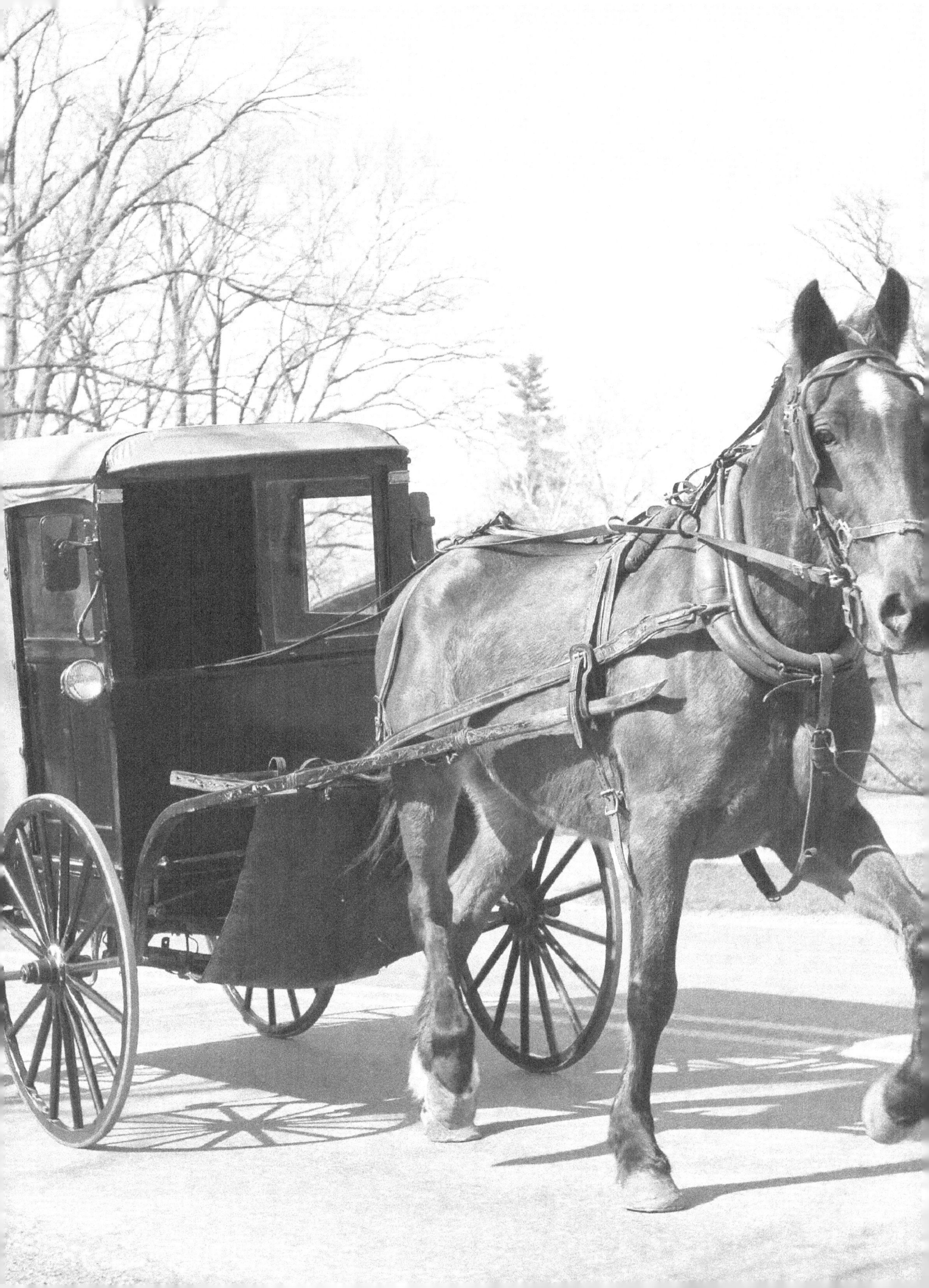

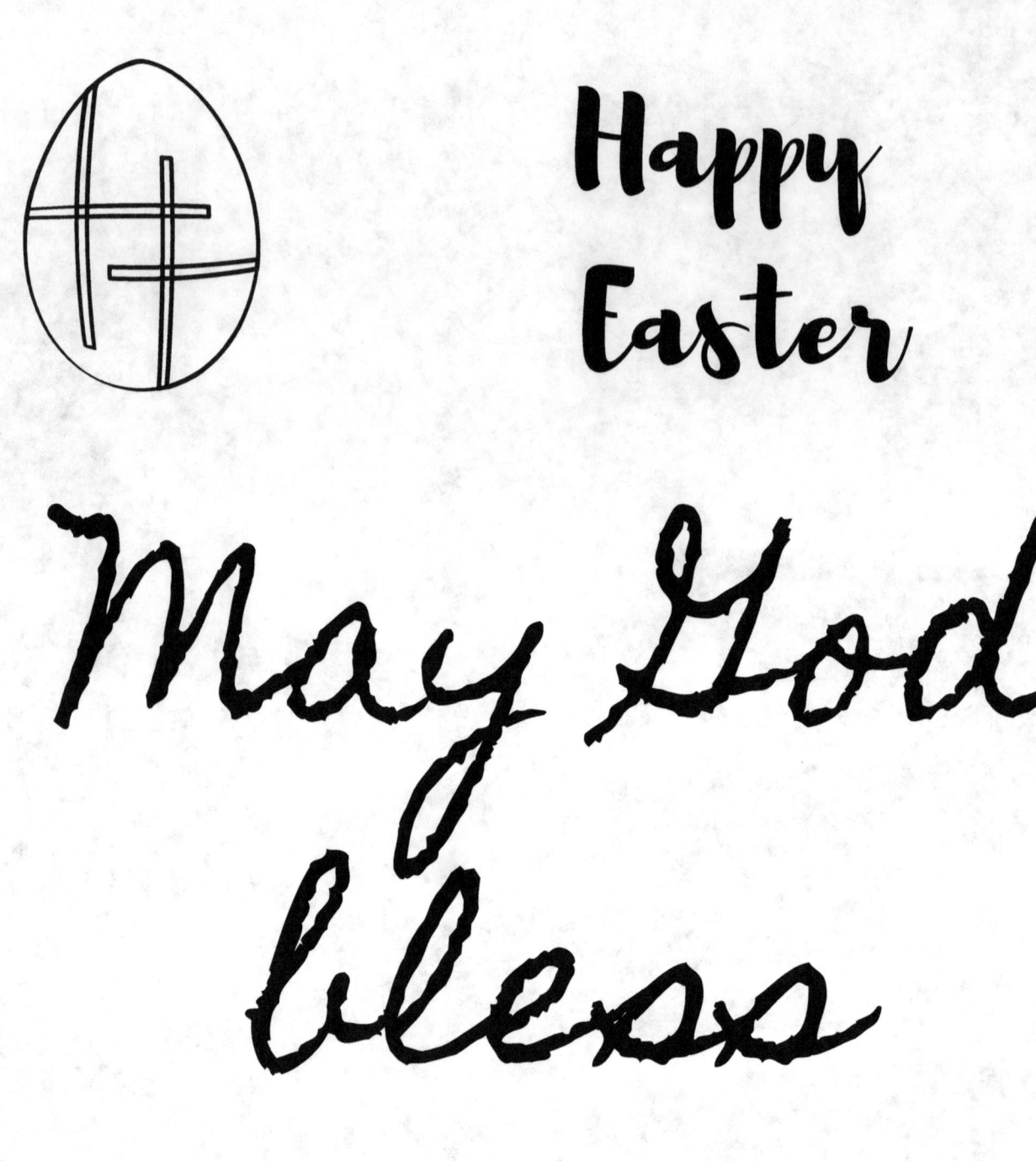

Happy Easter

May God bless you.

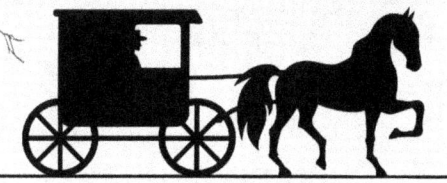

YOUR OPINION MATTERS TO ME!

Please let me know what you think of this book by leaving a review on the page you bought it from.

Just type this link into your browser to find the page: www.amzn.to/2JUGdTR

Thank you,
Mary

COUNT ME IN

www.ingramcontent.com/pod-product-compliance
Lightning Source LLC
Chambersburg PA
CBHW081459220526
45466CB00008B/2719